Judging the Authenticity of Prints by The Masters
a primer for collectors

* * * *

David Rudd Cycleback

cycleback.com

isbn: 978-0-6151-7185-2

2

Judging the Authenticity of Prints by The Masters
a primer for collectors
by David Rudd Cycleback

Publisher: Cycleback.com
isbn: 978-0-6151-7185-2

CONTENTS

(1)
INTRODUCTION

This guide is about making sound judgments concerning the authenticity, or lack thereof, of prints by famous artists, from Rembrandt to Andy Warhol. While a small book hardly intends to cover it all or make the reader into the next Sotheby's expert, it covers many of the essentials to making sound opinions.

This guide is a supplement to your personal experience and springboard to your continuing education. This experience and education includes handling and looking at a variety of prints, studying your area of interest, reading books and articles, researching, visiting museums and informational websites, and asking lots and lots of questions of dealers, experts and fellow collectors.

(2)
ESSENTIAL TIPS FOR BEGINNING COLLECTORS OF MOST ANYTHING

Whether it involves celebrity autographs, movie posters, fine art prints, baseball cards, postcards or vases, collecting can be good clean fun for boys and girls of all ages. However, all areas of collecting have fakes, reprints and scams.

The following is a brief but important list of tips that the beginner should read before jumping into the hobby with open pocketbook.

1) Start by knowing that there are reprints, counterfeits, fakes and scams out there. If you start by knowing you should be doing your homework, having healthy skepticism of sellers' grand claims and getting second opinions, you will be infinitely better off than the beginner who assumes everything's authentic and all sellers are honest.

2) Learn all you can about material you wish to collect and the hobby in general. The more you learn and more experience you have, the better off you are. Most forgers aren't trying to fool the knowledgeable. They're trying to fool the ignorant and gullible.

3) Realize that novices in any area of collecting are more likely to overestimate, rather than underestimate, the value of items they own or are about to buy.

4) Get second opinions and seek advice when needed. This can range from a formal opinion from a top expert to input from a collecting friend. Collectors who seek advice and input are almost always better off than those who are too proud or embarrassed to ask questions.

5) Start by buying inexpensive items. Put off the thousands dollar Babe Ruth baseball cards and Elvis Presley autographed photos for another day.

Without exception, all beginners make mistakes. From paying too much to misjudging rarity to buying fakes. It only makes sense that a collector should want to make the inevitable beginner's mistakes on $10 rather that $1,000 purchases.

9) Gather a list of good sellers. A good seller is someone who is knowledgeable and trustworthy. A good seller fixes a legitimate problem when it arises, and has a good authenticity guarantee and return policy.

It's best to buy real expensive items online from good sellers, including those you have dealt with and those who otherwise have strong reputations. Some of the sellers you purchase inexpensive items from will make your list of good sellers.

(3)
WHAT IS AUTHENTICITY?

In all areas of collecting, from movie memorabilia to oil paintings, something is authentic if its true identity is described accurately and sincerely.

If you pay good money for an "original 1930 Greta Garbo photograph by the famous Hollywood photographer George Hurrell," you expect to receive an original 1930 Greta Garbo photo by George Hurrell. You don't expect a 1970 reprint or a photo by an unknown photographer.

An item does not have to be rare or expensive or old to be authentic. It just has to be accurately and sincerely described. A cheapo 2003 reprint can be authentic if described as a cheapo 2003 reprint.

Errors in the description of an item are considered significant when they significantly affect the financial value or reasonable non-financial expectations of the buyer. An example of the reasonable non-financial expectations would involve a collector who specializes in real photo post cards of her home state of Iowa and makes it crystal clear to the seller that she only wants postcards depicting Iowa. Even if there is no financial issue, she would have reason to be disappointed if the purchased postcard turned out to show Oklahoma or Minnesota.

Many errors in description are minor and have little to no material effect. If that 1930 Greta Garbo photo turns out to be from 1934, it may not effect the financial value or desirability to the purchaser.

Common terms:

Counterfeit: a reprint or reproduction that is made to fool others into believing it is original.

Forgery: an item that was made to fool others into believing it is something it is not. This includes counterfeits, but also made up items, like a 'newly discovered' Rembrandt painting that never existed.

Fake: an item that is seriously misidentified. This includes forgeries and counterfeits. It also includes items that are innocently but badly misidentified by collectors or sellers who are uninformed.

When in doubt about seller's intent, it's best to call a bad sale or auction item a fake instead of a forgery or counterfeit. All three words mean an item is not genuine, but forgery and counterfeit implies intentional illegality.

It's about making judgments

This guide isn't about becoming omniscient or gaining superhero powers of authentication. It's about forming sound opinions based on your knowledge, experience, tools, resources and common sense.

With many prints you will be confident to certain they are genuine.

With many prints you will be confident to certain they are fakes or otherwise have significant errors in description.

A percentage of prints you won't be able to make a definitive opinion about. Perhaps the print is outside your area of specialty. Perhaps the print has something strange about it, but not strange enough to prove it fake.

There's nothing wrong with being unsure. Even the experts at Christie's and the Louver sometimes scratch their heads and seek outside opinions.

Judging authenticity is rarely done in a vacuum

For the collector, making judgments is usually done within a context. Usually the context is deciding whether or not to purchase and how much to pay.

A knowledgeable collector might take a wild chance on a foreign print if the price is $30 and it will look sharp on the wall, but pass if the price is $500. A collector might purchase an unfamiliar print if he knows the seller to be knowledgeable, but wouldn't give it a second glace if the seller had a reputation for selling fakes.

You never have to buy a work of art or piece of memorabilia. If you are uncomfortable with the looks of the item, the price or the reliability of the seller, you can choose not to bid or buy.

(4)
RESEARCHING THE ARTIST'S WORK:
THE CATALOGUE RAISONNE

For those concerned about identification and authentication of famous original art, *catalogues raisonne* are invaluable information sources. Catalogues raisonne (singular: catalogue raisonne) are large illustrated books used by major auction houses, museums and top dealers to help identify, date and authenticate prints. They are also a great starting point for the beginning collector, offering an illustrated survey and description of the artist's work.

A catalogue raisonne is a book or series of books covering either the artist's entire body of work or specific areas (paintings, sculpture, prints, area of prints). They are produced by the top experts in the field, including professors, gallery owners, museum curators and the artist's publishers. Input and approval is often given by the artist or artist's estate.

While catalogues raisonne vary in quality, a good one will be extensively illustrated and give most of the essentials of the artist's original prints. These essentials can include dimensions of a print, type of printing used (etching, engraving, other), number of prints, editions, how a print is signed and numbered, the type of paper used and so on. A catalogue often includes helpful biographical and artistic information, such as describing the printing techniques and styles. Some offer samples of the artist's signature. Some catalogues are so lavishly illustrated they are worth the price simply as coffee table books and can be enjoyed by non collectors.

The essentialness of a catalogue raisonne is that it shows what prints are recognized as genuine works by the artist. While there will be some legitimate uncatalogued prints, for the most part the collector should stick to what is catalogued. If a print for sale is not listed and detailed in a catalogue raisonne or called genuine by other substantive source (expert opinion, authoritative article), the collector should not buy.

If the least that collectors of the world did was to determine if a for sale print is listed as authentic in the catalogue raisonne and that the bare basics matches the catalogue listing (size, signature, numbering, etc), the sale of forgeries and fakes would be reduced by about 95%.

Obtaining a particular artist's catalogue can be difficult. While catalogues by some artist's can be bought at popular bookstores, they are sometimes expensive. Some are extremely difficult to find. Luckily, a growing number of catalogues are online for free, including those of Pablo Picasso, Marc Chagall and Andy Warhol.

For the hard to find catalogues raisonne, the collector should look high and low. This includes looking at used bookstores, libraries and asking around. Some galleries or dealers have libraries and will let collectors reference them.

In an online-auction description, a good seller will tell the bidders that a print is officially "listed" as genuine, by referencing the catalogue's title, author and the catalogue number for the print. This is a convenience for the bidders and will often boost the sales price.

Online Catalogues Raisonne and Information Sources:

John James Audubon: http://www.audubon.org/nas/art.html
    Brief but useful info page

Marc Chagall: http://chagall.fr

Leroy Neiman: http://www.leroyneiman.com
    Neiman's official site, maintained by his publisher. Includes commentary for collectors by the Neiman.

Pablo Picasso: http://www.tamu.edu/mocl/picasso

Andy Warhol : http://www.warholprints.com
  This site is maintained by a gallery that published many of
  Warhol's works. The information is endorsed by the
  Warhol estate.

 Winslow Homer's Harper's Woodcuts:
  http://www.sonofthesouth.net/Winslow_Homer.htm
  Not a comprehensive data source, but pictures all of
  Homer's prints for the popular 1800s magazine.

Gemini G.E.L. Online Catalogue Raisonne :
  http://www.nga.gov/gemini/home.htm
  Famous printing house, gives great detail on prints made by
  their famous printers including Warhol and Lichtenstein.
  Detailed images.

Titles Search:
The Print Council Index to Oeuvre-Catalogues of Prints by
European and American Artists. This lists about all of the
catalogues raisonne ever published:
http://www.printcouncil.org/search.html

 Online Booksellers:
 Barnes and Noble http://www.bn.com
 Amazon http://www.amazon.com
 Alibris http://www.alibris.com (Specializes in rare books, so
 offers a larger selection)
 eBay http://www.ebay.com (Check regularly, and you will
 often see rare catalogues for auction.)

 Other information sources:
 http://www.askart.com
 http://www.artnet.com
 http://www.artdealers.org

(5)
PRINTING: INTRODUCTION

The identification and understanding of printing is an essential part of judging authenticity. It only makes sense that if you want to judge the authenticity of a Rembrandt etching, you should be able to tell what an etching looks like. A large percentage of fakes are made with printing processes inconsistent with the original. A reproduction of a woodcut may be a lithograph. A forgery of a lithograph may be home computer print.

Even if you never become a printing expert, with experience you can make reasonable judgments about printing. For example, it is simple to identify many fakes and reprints by looking at the printing pattern with a magnifying glass.

Beyond authentication and forgery detection, being able to identify and understand prints makes viewing and collecting art more enjoyable.

Being able to identify and date printing requires knowing how a type of printing looks both in its general appearance and under the microscope or magnifying glass. For up close examination, I recommend a microscope of 30x to 100x power. Handheld examples can be purchased at eBay, amazon.com and elsewhere for well under $20.

The following chapters are an introduction to identifying many of the major processes. These chapters are a guide to your hands-on study and observations.

Making your own prints
Throughout the printing chapters, you will be shown how to

make prints at home. Making prints is instructional towards the understanding and identification of prints. It can also be good, clean fun. All the techniques shown are straight foreword. Kids are encouraged to join in, though parents should oversee where sharp instruments and messy inks are used.

(6)
WHAT IS A PRINT?

By tradition, printing is the making of an image in ink by pressing an inked printing plate (steel plate, block of wood, other) onto paper or other material. The paper or other material instead can be pressed against the printing plate. The printing surface (the surface of the printing plate where the ink is placed) must be in a form that can print the same image many times. The resulting image on paper or other material is a print.

An example of printing that most of us have had experience with is the rubber stamp. I own one that prints my mailing address on envelopes and documents. The printing surface of a rubber stamp is in a shape that it can print the image over and over, as long as there's enough ink in the inkpad.

There have been hundreds of different kinds of printing processes. Some are ancient and hand made, some use the latest computer technology. With the change in technology, the definition of printing has been bent. Some modern printing processes don't use printing plates, at least not in the traditional sense. Screen printing, known as silk screen in the United States, involves the forcing of ink thought a screen. Inkjet computer printers squirt ink onto the paper. Some computer printers don't even use ink. While these and other processes don't follow the rules of tradition, they can be considered prints in a broader sense. Master printmaker Gabor Peturdi put it well when he the wrote, "Because these (non traditional) processes represent an important development that may ultimately replace the other processes, printing should probably now be defined as any of several techniques for reproducing texts and illustrations, in black and in color, on a durable surface and in a desired number of identical copies."

What is not a print?
Related things that are not prints include paintings, drawings and photographs. In painting and drawing there is no printing plate that can be used to make multiple images. The image is created directly on the paper, canvas or other by hand. A painting or drawing is by nature unique.

In ways, photographic prints are similar to prints. A negative (a transparent sheet of glass, plastic or other material with the photographic image in negative on the surface) is made by the photographer and this negative can be used to *print* many photographs. Photography does not use ink. A photographic image is created by the interaction of chemically treated paper and light. Amongst collectors and historians, photography is considered a different genre than ink and printing press inks. Most collectors, dealers and historians make a clear distinction between prints and photographs.

(7)
HAND MADE VERSUS
PHOTOMECHANICAL PRINTS

Prints can be divided into many different categories, including by they way that they are made, what materials are used, whether they are commercial or non-commercial, and artistic styles. For this book, an essential category is whether prints are **hand made** or **photomechanical**. These two categories often distinguish a print from being original and reproduction.

Hand made prints are made from printing plates whose artistic design is created onto the plate by hand. An original Rembrandt engraving involved the famous artist literally using a hand held tool to carve the design into the steel plate. A wood-engraving was made by someone cutting the artistic design into a block of wood by hand.

Photomechanical prints are the opposite of hand made prints. The design on the printing plate is through photographic reproduction, not by hand. Photomechanical prints are most commonly used for mass-production commercial purposes, including making reprints of hand made prints. With notable exceptions, all twentieth century and today's commercial prints are photomechanical prints. This includes everything from the images on trading cards to cereal boxes, movie posters to magazines. These commercial prints involve the reproduction of an original design, whether it's a painting, photograph, print or sketch.

Hand made prints printed by or directly overseen and approved by the artist are commonly called 'original prints' in the fine arts world. Most photomechanical reprints, even if approved of by the artist, are not considered original.

The concept of originality, with all its degrees and gray areas, is discussed more in a later chapter.

(8)
HAND MADE PRINTS :
THREE SUB CATEGORIES

This chapter discusses some of the standard categories essential to the understanding and identification of printing and prints.

The Three Types of Printing:
Relief, Intaglio and Planographic
All traditional printing belongs to one of three general types: relief, intaglio or planographic. The difference between these types is in a combination of the form of the printing plate and how the ink lays on or in the plate. These differences show up in the final print, including its general appearance.

A **relief** print is made by cutting away part of the surface of the printing plate, adding ink to the raised surface that is left and pressing the plate surface to the paper. The area that was cut away will not appear on the paper, while the area that was left will. If you take a block of wood, carve your initials into it, ink it up and press it on a piece of paper, you have made a relief print. Everything but your initials will appear on the paper. If you had instead cut away everything except your initials, it would print just your initials. Examples of relief printing include the woodcut, wood-engraving and linoleum cut.

Intaglio printing also involves cutting away part of the surface of a printing plate. The difference from relief is that the ink is placed in the lower parts, or recesses, of the plate. During the printing process it takes great pressure to get the ink from the recesses onto the paper. Examples of intaglio printing include engraving, etching and dry point.

Planographic printing involves a flat printing plate with the ink lying on the surface. As detailed later on, special substances placed on the plate surface isolate the ink into the desired image. The most common form of this printing is lithography.

Miscellaneous. There are a number of processes that are not traditional. Some are barely prints at all. These include the monoprint and cliche-verre.   These are, however, popularly included in the genre of prints.

(9)
HAND MADE PRINTS: RELIEF

Due to the way that relief prints are made, the ink has a distinct look under the microscope. The printing often has a dark rim around the edge of the ink. In cases, this can be seen with the naked eye or ordinary magnifying glass. This rim appears on all types of relief prints, both hand made and photomechanical (see photoengraving in later chapter). The only non-relief print that sometimes has a similar rim is early chromolithography (a colorful form of lithography). However, this rim in chromolithography is cause by the settling of the thin lithographic ink and will appear more irregular than mechanical. In relief printing the ink is most apparent on smooth, glossy paper. If the paper is rough, such as with newsprint or hand made paper, the rim may not be a noticeable.

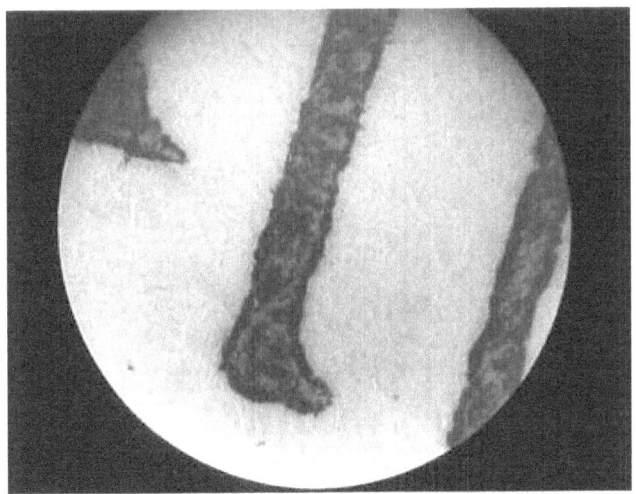

100X power view of the a relief print
showing typical rim or edge around the ink

As a relief print is made by the pressure of the printing plate against the printing surface, some relief prints will have an embossment on the back of the paper. This can often be felt with the fingertips and seen. If the paper is thick or there is printing on the back, such as with the pages of a book, the embossment may not be apparent.

The following pages cover the major types of hand made relief prints.

WOODCUT

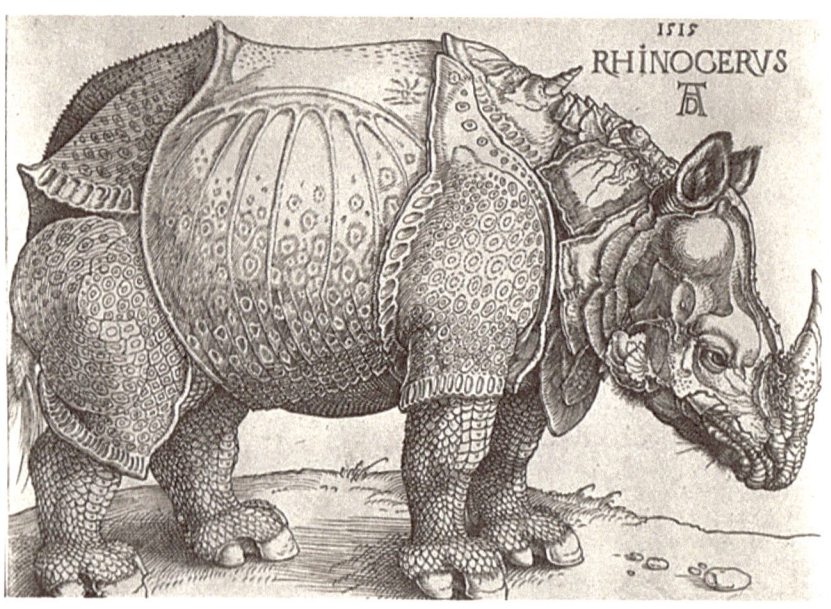

1515 woodcut by Albrecht Durer. The date, title and Durer's monogram are in the upper right, printed with the rest of the graphics.

The relief print called woodcut is both the name for the printing process and the print itself. The artist or craftsman carves the design into the plank side of the wood using chisels, gouges and similar tools.

The woodcut is an ancient form of printing, used in ancient China. It flourished in Europe after the 14th century. During the 17th and 18th century the Japanese made influential woodcuts. The woodcut was commonly used for commercial prints until the mid 1800s, when it was replaced by wood-engraving, a finer type of woodcut. The woodcut has used by many famous artists, including Albrecht Durer, Pablo Picasso and Salvador Dali.

Identification. Along with the dark rim around the ink that is typical to relief printing, the woodcut is identified because of the distinct and often primitive lines .The white areas are the result of the wood being scooped from the block. If you can imagine the white areas being scooped out, then this is a strong indication it is a woodcut. Two other types of prints can resemble the woodcut: wood-engraving (a form of woodcut, linoleum cut and photoengraving (photomechanical primarily used for mass production in the early to mid 20th century).

Due to the natural irregular shape of the wood, neither the woodcut nor the wood-engraving can print large areas of solid ink without showing the grain or irregular shape of the wood. To simulate large areas of solid color, a series of parallel or cross-hatching lines was made. These lines will appear as white light lines against the area of otherwise solid ink.

The linoleum cut often closely resembles a woodcut. One of the most noticeable differences between the two is that the linoleum cut can print large areas of solid ink.

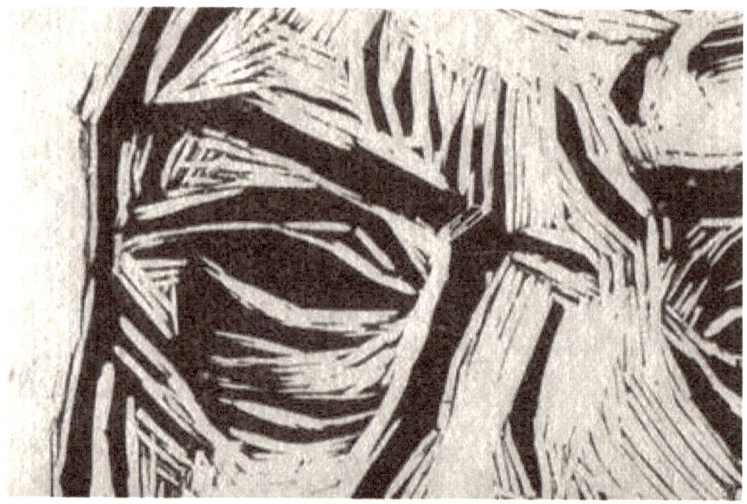

detail of a woodcut revealing how the block of wood was carved

WOOD-ENGRAVING

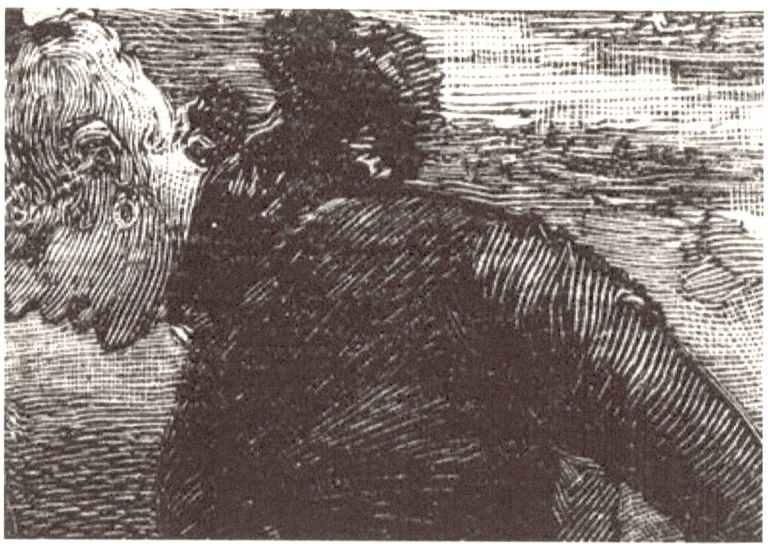

Wood-engraving is a form of woodcut that largely replaced the woodcut for mass production commercial purposes in the mid

1800s. It was the common way to make pictures for newspaper and magazines until the 1890s when it was slowly replaced by photoengraving. In the fine arts, wood-engravings are still made today.

A harder wood is used than with the woodcut, and the artist carves across the grain of the wood (*end-grain*). This allows for finer and more detailed lines on the block of wood and in the resulting print.

Identification: As with all relief prints, the wood engraving has the hard rim around the ink that can be viewed under the microscope and sometimes with the naked eye. It sometimes has an embossment on the back of the print caused by the printing pressure. The wood-engraving can closely resemble the woodcut in general appearance, except that the wood-engraving is more detailed with finer lines. If the white line is thin and delicate, it is most probably a wood-engraving instead of a woodcut. It was not possible to create such a fine line in the woodcut.

Due to the natural irregular shape of the wood, neither the woodcut or wood-engraving could print large areas of solid ink without showing the grain of the wood. To simulate large areas of solid color, a series of parallel or cross-hatching lines was often made.

METAL CUT AND RELIEF ETCHING

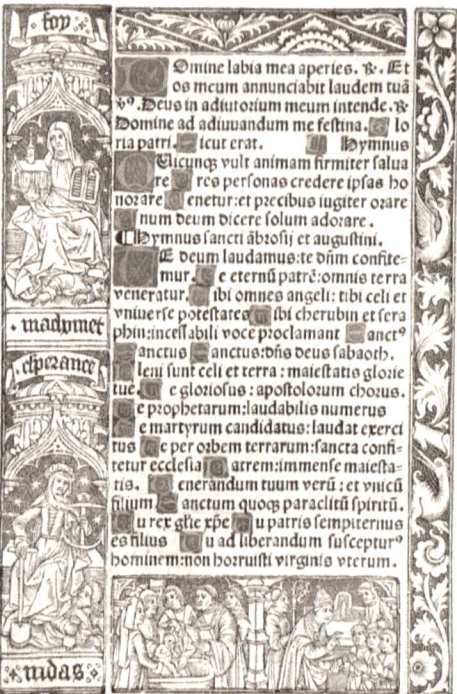

centuries old book page with metal cut design surrounding the text

There are various hand made relief printing methods that use metal instead of wood. The most frequent method is to cut a metal plate in the same way as cutting wood. This was frequently done from the fifteenth to nineteenth century for decorations, such as border illustrations and designs in books. With some early prints it is impossible to determine whether a print was made by wood or metal.

In the fifteenth century, the outline of the design was often engraved, then the area within stamped and punched. These are called manière criblée or *in the dotted manner* and have a distinct, primitive look.

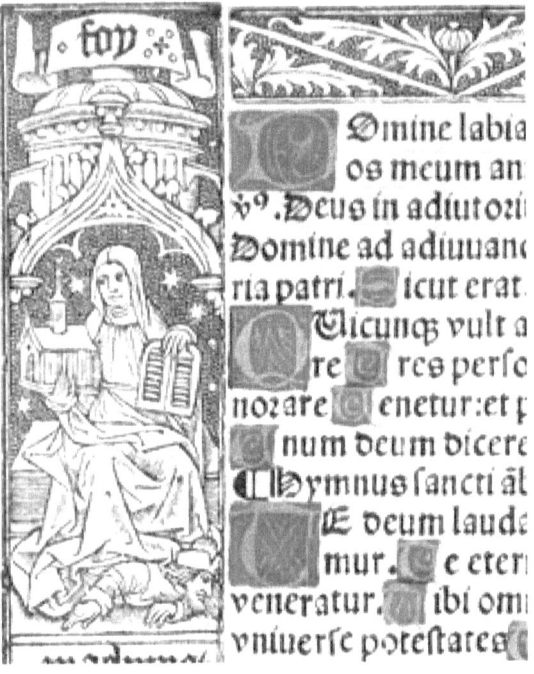

detail of earlier book page

The British poet and printer William Blake made the pictures for his books using etched metal plates printed in the relief form. The prints were either printed in color or hand-colored, and original prints have unique color variations from book to book.

LINOLEUM CUT

The linoleum cut, also known as linocut and linoleum block, is a twentieth century invention. Through introduced at the beginning of the 1900s, it was not popularized with artists until Pablo Picasso and Henri Matisse used it in the 1950s. Since then, it has been commonly used by artists.

The linoleum is made just like a woodcut, except a block of linoleum is used instead of wood. Linoleum is cheap and, unlike wood, soft and easy to cut. Many of us have made linoleum cuts in school or at home. As linoleum is easier to cut, a linocut can have many different effects, lines and squiggles not possible with woodcuts.

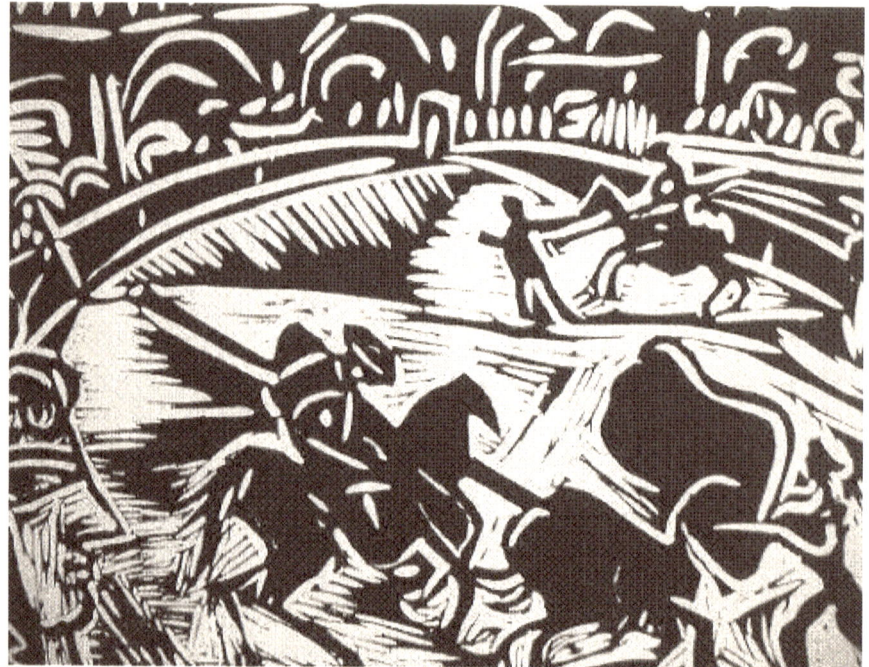

Detail of a Pablo Picasso Linocut

Linoleum cuts often look like woodcuts. It is sometimes difficult to tell if a print is linoleum cut or a woodcut. As with most relief prints, the linocut has a noticeable rim around the ink. Due to the smooth surface of the linoleum, linoleum cuts can print large areas of solid ink. This is unlike the woodcut, which cannot print large areas of solid color.

MAKING YOUR OWN RELEIF PRINTS
There is a wide variety of relief prints that you can make at home, using a variety of materials. This section is an introduction to a few common forms and techniques. It will introduce the concept of color printing and reductive printing

color.

POTATOCUT

The potatocut, often called a potato print, is probably the simplest and easiest relief print to make. They can be made by both adults and kids. As potatoes are soft, only a butter or plastic knife is needed to cut the design into the potato. Despite its seeming simplicity, a wide range of designs and prints can be made.

Materials needed:
Potatoes
Knives
Printing ink or paint (paint usually dries faster)
Paper towel
Brush
Paper plate
Paper

Directions for making a monotone potatocut
1) Cut the potato in half. Make sure that the cut surface is as flat/smooth as possible.

2) Using the butter or plastic knife, cut your design into the surface. Some people prefer to draw the design into the potato surface. When carving, the surface that is left behind will be what is printed and the design on the potato will be printed in reverse. So if you want to print your initial, you will have to carve it is backwards. This cut surface is the printing surface, or where the ink will be added.   Since it's only a potato and you likely have others available as backups, start with a simple design to see how it works. As the printing surface of the potato is probably wet, dry it off with the paper towel. Extra moisture can interact with the ink or paint.

3) Put your desired color of ink or paint on a paper plate.

4) Either press the potato into the ink/paint, or use a brush to paint the ink onto the printing surface.

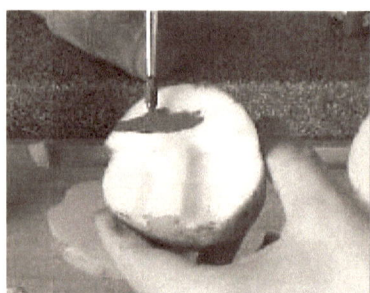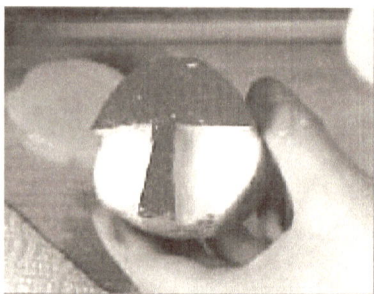

painting on the printing surface of the potato

5) To make the print, press the inked printing surface to the paper, like you would do with a rubber stamp. Press firmly, to make sure enough ink gets onto the paper. Make sure to not smudge the print. Lift the potato and you have made a potato print.

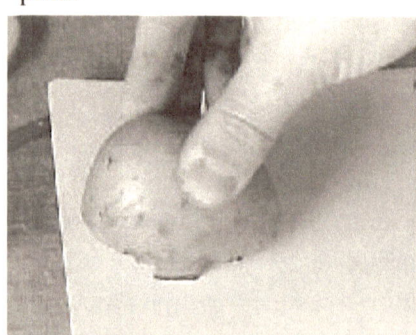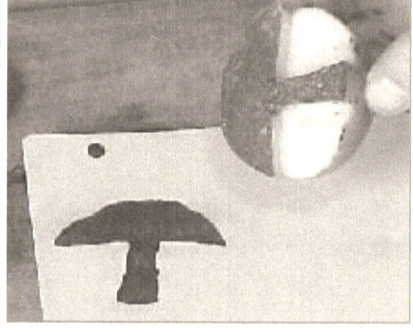

 6) If you don't like the way the print works out, try it again with the same or new ink. If you don't like the design, either carve some more into the potato or try with a new potato. You can mix and match your different potato designs and colors to make a wide variety of designs. You can also add hand coloring, to fix mistakes or add details (this would now be called a 'potatocut with hand coloring' or 'mixed media potatocut' because you have mixed the potatocut with hand coloring). Potato cuts are great for kids to make greeting cards and even T-shirts.

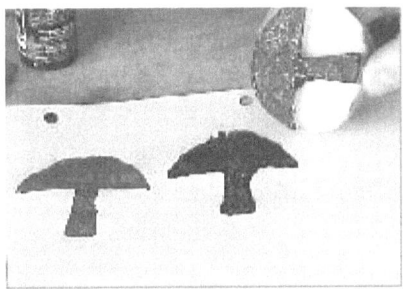

* * * *

Making a Color Potato Print

The traditional way to make a color print is from multiple printing plates, one plate for each color. You can make a color potatocut this way.

To start, you might wish to make a two color potatocut, from two potato halves. Before carving your design, you should think about what colors you want and what designs you will make. It's usually best, at least when beginning, to start with the background in a light color, then the second print will be the details. For example, the first potato half may print a solid light blue background, perhaps with a small cutout cloud in the background. The second print then might print a black tree or dog or whatever. Most printers will wait for the first color to dry before printing the second color. Others like the effect of printing while the first color is still wet. Once you have your two potatocuts, you can print as many prints as you wish, including in different color combinations. Some artists will add a bit of hand painting in order to add details or fix printing mistakes.

The Reductive Color Potato Print

Reductive printing is a unique and brain-challenging way to make a color print. It is usually used with the linocut ('reductive linocut'), and is most commonly found in the fine arts. Pablo Picasso produced some of the most famous examples.

In reductive printing, there is only one printing plate (one potato half). After using the plate to print the first color, the artist carves out more of the plate and prints the second color, then carves more of the plate and prints the third color, and so on for each additional color. Especially with complicated designs, this type of printing takes great planning, because there is no turning back.

There are reasons an artist makes reductive prints, other than the fun and challenge of it. One is that you don't have to deal with the hassle and cost of making several printing plates. Also, since you are working from a single plate, carving away as you go, it is easy to make sure your deigns and proportions match.

Directions for Reductive Potato Print

1) Cut the potato in half. The cut surface should be as smooth/flat as possible. Use the towel to wipe off the extra moisture, as the water may not interact well with the paint or ink. This flat cut surface is the printing surface' meaning where the ink will go.

2) This smooth surface will be your first color, giving the background color. Add a light color ink or paint to the printing surface, like yellow or beige. Press the printing surface onto the piece of paper, making sure not to smudge the print. You should make a few prints, adding more ink if necessary. Remember, since this is a reductive print, there's no going back if you make a mistake.

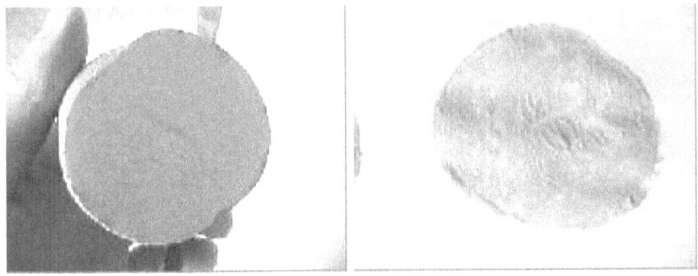

3) Remove the ink from the printing surface and carve out part of the printing surface for the next color. Add the second color paint or ink to the new printing surface. The color should be darker, like blue or red or green. Press the printing surface over the first color. Make sure that everything is lined up and the potato is in the same position (top of design is on top again, etc). If you make a mistake lining up the print, you will realize why I recommended you make more than one print at the start.

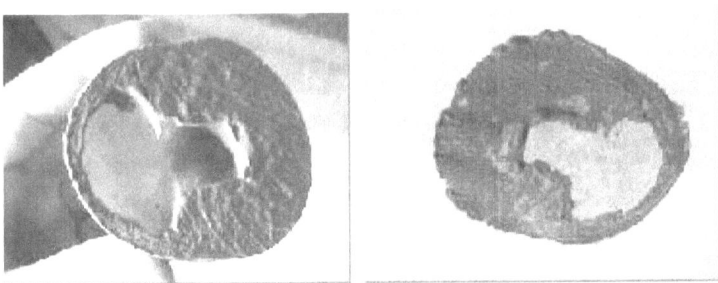

4) Remove the ink from the printing surface and carve away more of the printing surface. This last printing surface will usually produce the dark outline or other last details. Add black or other very dark ink to the surface and print this on the paper.

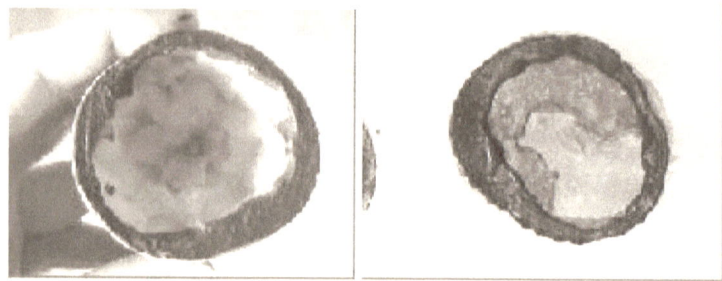

5) You have made a reductive print.

Using Other Materials

Relief prints can be made from a variety of commonly found material, including wood, linoleum, cardboard, erasures and other vegetables. All of these materials can be cut or altered in similar ways as the potato. You can also relief print many ready-made printing plates, including old coins, bones, stones and keys.

Linoleum is commonly used in the fine arts. It is relatively inexpensive and easy to use. Linoleum comes in sheets or in blocks (a sheet of linoleum pasted to a block of wood). To put your design into the linoleum, you will need special linoleum cutters. These are handheld tools with different sized heads. They can be bought in many art and craft stores and catalogs. You may also wish to get an ink roller, which is a hand held roller that evenly applies the ink. As linoleum is larger, smoother and harder, you will find you can made more intricate and larger prints than with the potato.

At this point, you will probably find it best to print in a different way than with the potatocut. Instead of stamping you printing plate down onto the paper, you can press the paper down onto the printing plate. With the paper onto top of the inked printing surface, even apply pressure by rubbing your hand, towel or a tool called a brayer. You then remove the paper, by slowly peeling it from one corner. It you lift it suddenly straight up, the ink might smudge.

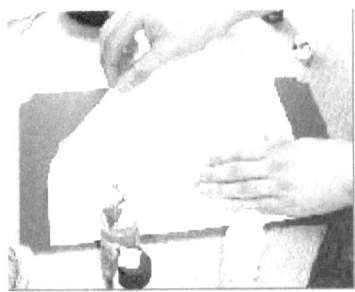

**applying pressure to the paper on the printing
plate, and removing the paper from the plate**

A woodcut is made in basically the same way as a linocut, except wood is used instead of linoleum. Special cutters for wood can be bought at stores. When cutting the wood, it is not necessary to cut deeply into the wood to make a print.

(10)
HAND MADE INTAGLIO PRINTS

As a general category, intaglio prints are identified by several qualities caused by the unique way they are printed. These qualities include the following:

Plate mark: Many intaglio prints have a plate mark a distance away from the printed image. These appear as an indentation around the printed image the shape of the printing plate. Many times the printed image is pressed deep into the paper. The plate mark is caused by the great pressure required to get the ink from the recesses and onto the paper. Sometimes the plate mark edges are trimmed from the print. On some occasions, plate marks may appear naturally on other types of printing or are faked.

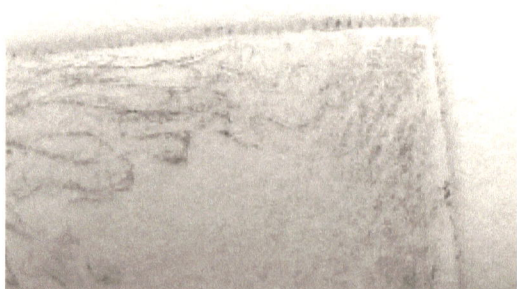

The pressed in 'plate mark' on a dry point

Raised ink levels. Unlike relief and lithography, the ink on an intaglio print can be physically raised from the paper. This is because the ink comes from inside the recesses of the printing plate. To make dark areas of a print, the printing plate is cut deeper to allow thicker ink. In the lighter areas of a print, the cut in the printing plate is shallow. This means that the physical height of the ink in an intaglio is most easily detected in the areas of dark ink. Sometimes the ink can be felt by softly rubbing a finger across the printing or by looking very closely with the naked eye. In other cases, a microscope is needed. If the paper surface is rough, it may be difficult to identify.

Varying tone within a line: Within a single line or mark, planography and relief can only create one tone of ink. Due to the varying levels of ink applied, the tone along an intaglio line can vary, meaning it can become darker or lighter.

Intaglio plates tend to wear with printing, resulting in prints in different states (see Chapter: *States*). This places a limit on the number of prints that can be made from the plate.

The following are different common types of intaglio:

ENGRAVING

Engraving was the first form of intaglio printing, invented in the early 1400s.

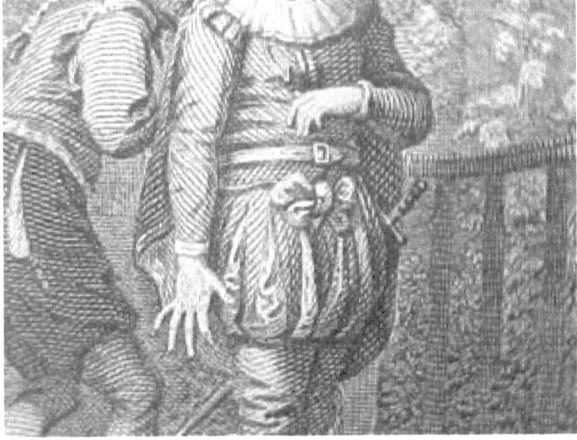

the typical formal style of lines in an engraving

In engraving, the engraver carves a design into a steel or copper plate. The carving tool is called a burin and has a sharp V-shaped section. The engraver holds the burin almost parallel with the plate, pressing the point into the surface and scooping out a sliver of metal. This is difficult work and the result is a conservative, steady line with crisp edges. The line also tends to be pointed at each end where the burin is first dipped into the copper the lifted out at the other end. If the engraver goes back over the line, the 'v' ending can be blunted, but usually at least one edge has a pointed, v shape.

Engraving is usually made up of many parallel lines and curves. There are different ways to give an appearance of tone. One way is to lessen or increase the pressure of the burin when carving the line. This makes the line thinner in some areas and wider in others. Engraving can also have cross-hatched lines, sometimes with dots or flicked spots added to the middles of the resulting diamonds. This is called the *dot and lozenge* technique. There is also stipple engraving which is discussed later.

Identification. Along with the general intaglio traits (physically raised ink, plate mark. etc), engraving has a formal look created by the stoic and controlled lines. Etching is more spontaneous, like a sketch.

ETCHING

Etching is a form of intaglio printing that first appeared in the early 1500s. Etching was easier than engraving for the artist. With engraving, the artist has to perform the difficult task of cutting the grooves into the steel plate. With etching, the artist draws the art onto the plate, then acid creates the grooves in the plate. Not only does this make it easier on the artist, but the final print has a different, freer look than engraving.

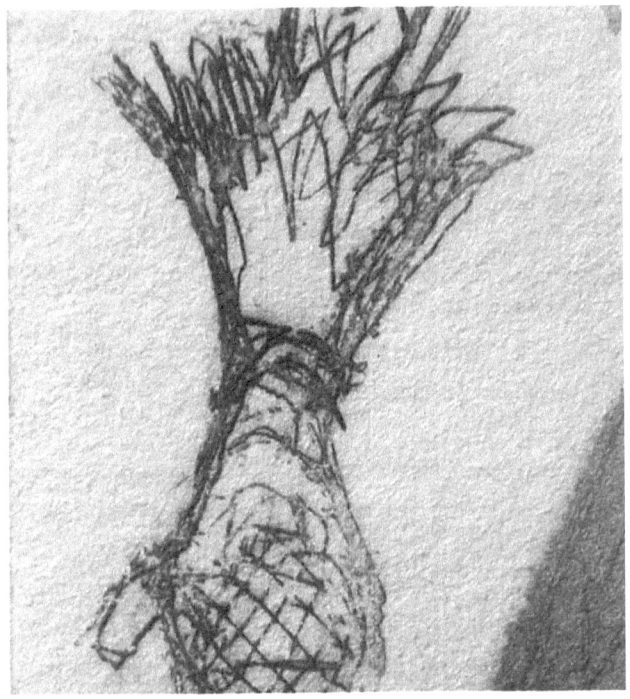

detail of an etching showing free, sketch-like lines

The etching process is as follows. The metal printing plate is heated and wax is rubbed over the surface to create a thin and even coating. This coating is known as the ground. After it is cooled and hardened, the ground is impervious to acid. If acid was poured on the ground, the plate would be unmarked. The etcher creates lines or other marks through the ground, exposing the plate in these areas. When the plate is submerged in acid, the acid will eat away those exposed areas. The longer the plate is submerged, the deeper and broader a line will become, and the darker the printed line. By varying the length of exposure of one area over another, the etcher can change the comparative darkness. Commonly, the etcher will place varnish on areas that are dark enough, preventing any more acid exposure. This is called stopping out. After stopping out, the unvarnished areas are exposed more, making them darker. This stopping out can be done numerous times, allowing for subtle lines. Another way to create different types of lines is to add lines in the ground after the others have already been made. The later lines will be lighter, while the earlier ones will be darker.

Retrousage was a method of creating tone on the final print by not wiping away all the ink from the upper surface of the plate. Often a feather was used to tease some of the ink from the recesses lines onto the plate surface. This often appears on the final print as shading.

Etching was commonly used with other processes, including engraving and dry point.

Identification. Along with the general intaglio traits (physically raised ink, plate mark, etc), etching has the following specific traits. While engraving is known for its stoic careful lines, etching has much more freely drawn lines. Etchings often resemble ink sketches.

Etching uses a rounded needle to make the line, and the end should be more blunt than the sharp end of an engraving. The edges of the line should be less clean than that of an engraving. The combination of the crumbling wax and acid can create uneven edges.

STIPPLE ENGRAVING, CRAYON ENGRAVING, CHALK ENGRAVING

These techniques are commonly used with engraving and etching. Similar appearing techniques were used in other process, most notably lithography. These are centuries old techniques that are still used today by artists.

Stipple. The stipple technique was first used in engraving in the 1500s, and was later used in other types of printing including etching. Stipple engravings were especially popular around the turn of the 19th century. Stipple involves using many dots or small marks of varying size and shape to create tonal areas not possible with lines alone. Various tools could be used to make the marks in the plate. Often times both engraving and etching were used together. For example, the general design could be made with etching, then the stipple mark could be engraved. In general, the engraved stipple dot will look more like a flick, or short line, while the etched stipple mark will be more like a dot.

Crayon or chalk manner engravings. Though called engraving, this is more often used in etching. This technique gives the appearance of a crayon or chalk drawing. A tool called a roulette is used. The roulette is a metal wheel with sharp points that created a seemingly random series of dots along a line, which appeared much like a chalk line. Different sized roulettes produced different effects.

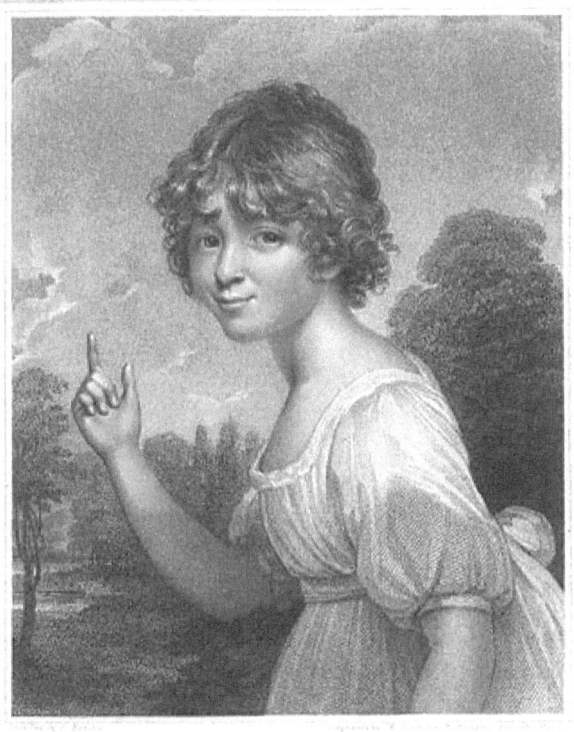

stipple engraving showing more tone than a normal engraving

MEZZOTINT

Also known as black manner, mezzotint is a form of intaglio printing that produces subtle and rich gradations in tone not possible with most other forms of manual intaglio. It was invented in the 1600s.

While engraving and etching can create only light or dark at a specific point, Mezzotint can create black, white and any shade in between. Mezzotints often have a rich, black velvety look. It was used alone or with other intaglio prints. For example, etching may be used to create the basic outline, while mezzotint is used to create the shading.

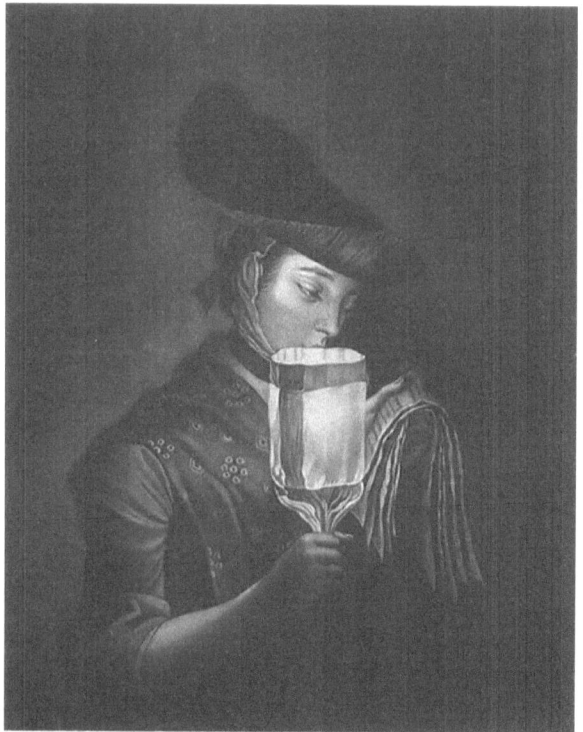

The distinct rich, velvety, white-out-of-black look of a mezzotint

The printing plate is created by pricking the surface with many, many tiny holes that hold ink, and make large areas of dark tone during printing. Different tools can be used to prick the plate. A roulette is a small wheel with sharp points. A rocker is a tool with a toothed edge that, when cutting the plate, creates rough edges. These edges are called burs. The burs are scraped away in places intended to be white in the finished print.

The mezzotint is identified by the thin and often cross-hatching lines in the grey tones. These are made from the scraping of the toothed edge tool. These lines also appear at the edges of the print. The mezzotint will typically have plate marks and raised ink levels typical to intaglio prints. Early mezzotint plates were prone to heavy wear. This means that later prints can be substantially lighter than earlier ones.

In the twentieth century new methods have been used. Many of these look like old mezzotints, but lack the richness and do not have the just described lines in the grays.

DRYPOINT

Dry point is an engraving method. A pointy tool scratches the design into the metal printing plate. This scratching often throws up a ridge of metal on the edges of the scratched line. This ridge is called a burr. When ink is added to the plate, the burr will hold ink, often giving the printed line a distinct fuzziness. This fuzziness can disappear over several printings. Due to the violent nature of the scratching into metal, the dry point line is often violent and angular. Dry point is most often used with other printmaking techniques.

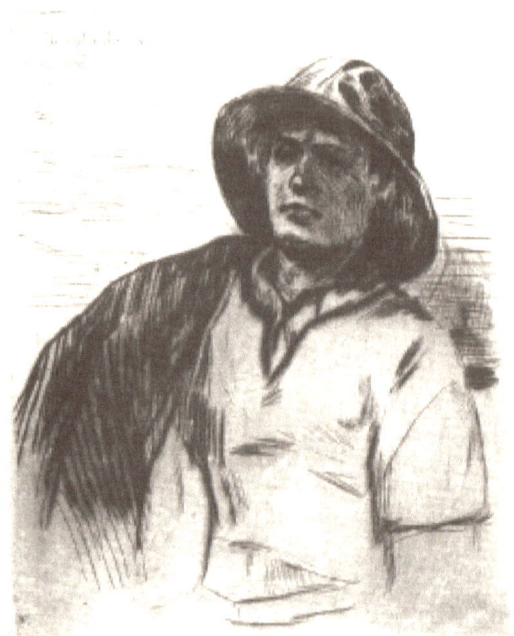

**The violent, angular lines of a drypoint,
with areas of heavy ink from the bur**

Dry point was first popularized in the late 15th century and is used by modern artists. As with other intaglio prints, it will usually have a plate mark surrounding the image.

AQUATINT

Aquatint is a variety of etching techniques used by printmakers to make a wide range of tonal effects. The prints often resemble wash sketches. The technique consists of exposing the metal printing plate to acid through a layer of granulated resin or sugar. The acid bites away the metal only in the spaces between the resin or sugar grains, leaving an evenly pitted surface that creates broad areas of tone when the plate is printed. An infinite number of tones can be achieved by exposing various parts of the plate to acid baths of different strengths for different periods of time. Etched or engraved lines are often used with aquatint. As with all intaglio prints, an aquatint will ordinarily have plate mark surrounding the image..

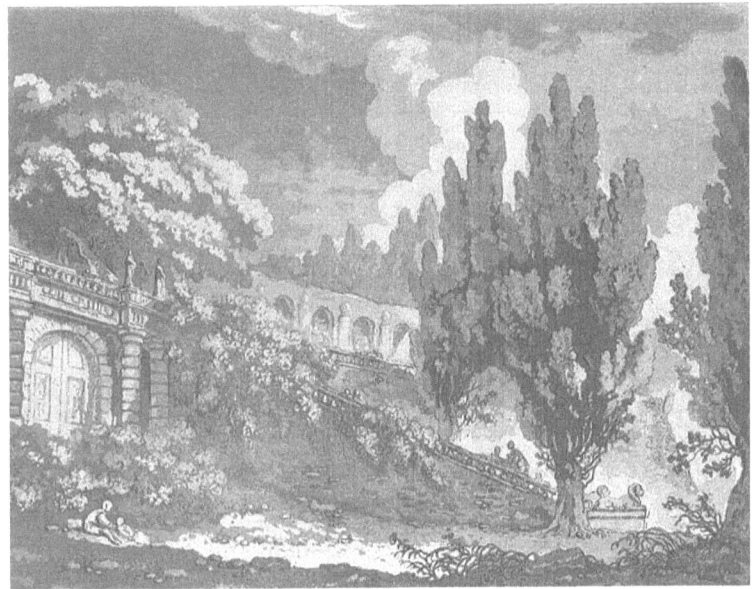

many tones of an aquatint

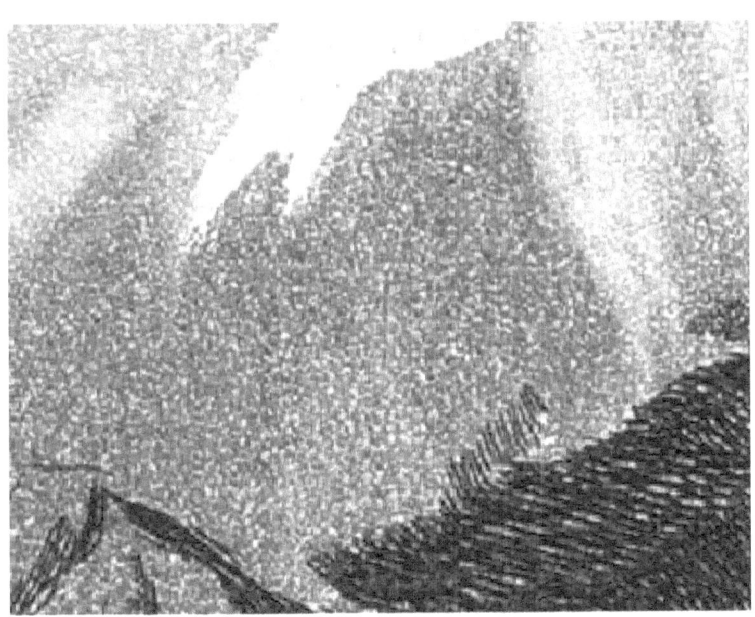

close up of a Goya aquatint

MAKING YOUR OWN INTAGLIO PRINTS

Due to special printing requirements, making intaglio prints is more difficult to do at home. In particular, a high amount of pressure is needed during printing which necessitates a printing press for consistent results. However, the reader who wants to experiment is welcome to try, and may end up make nice prints.

For a printing plate you can use linoleum. You might wish to start with one you already designed to make a linocut. Or you can start with a new one. When you ink up the printing plate, realize that the ink goes into the cut areas and not on the top surface like with a relief print. For printing, you need especially soft, absorbent paper. This is so the paper can go into the recesses of the printing plate without tearing. The paper should also be damp. Good paper is available at many art stores, but you can practice with a piece of soft paper towel.

During printing, there are two requirements. First, great pressure is needed. Second a soft cushion is needed in between this pressure and the paper. The printing presses that artists use have soft blankets as the cushion. The blankets press the paper into the recesses in inked areas, make sure the printing pressure is applied smoothly and evenly, and helps prevent the paper from tearing. When more pressure is used, more blankets are often used. At home you can use a variety of materials as the cushion, including a soft bath towel or other cloth or a roll of paper towel. As these materials may get inky, make sure to used old material you don't mind having to throw away.

(11)
HAND MADE LITHOGRAPHY

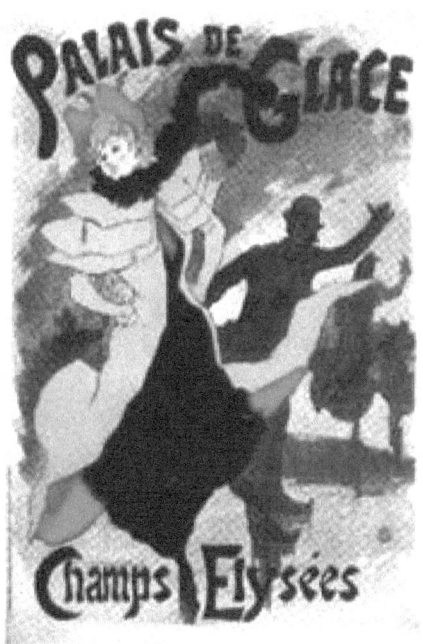

As lithography uses a flat printing plate, the resulting print lacks the distinct identification signs of relief (rim of ink) and intaglio (physically raised ink surface and plate mark). Even under the microscope, the ink on a lithograph lies flat and smooth on the printing surface. The lack of a distinct marking is what identifies it as planographic.

Handmade lithography has been popular in both the fine and 1800s commercial arts. Artists including Marc Chagall, Andy

Warhol and Salvador Dali have used the process. Today, photomechanical (not hand made) lithography is used to print everything from magazines and books to soup can labels and postcards.

Lithography was invented in 1778 Germany. The processed is based on the principle that water and grease do not mix. On a suitable flat printing surface marks are made in a greasy medium. The surface is dampened with water, which settles only on the unmarked areas as it is repelled by the greasy drawing medium. Next, a roller covered with greasy printing ink is rolled over the surface. The ink now adheres only to the drawn marks, the water repelling it from the rest of the surface. Finally, the ink is transferred to a sheet of paper by running paper and the printing surface together through a special press.

From the beginning European artists were intrigued with lithography, as they could draw and paint directly onto the printing plate. In the early 19th century lithography was usually monotone and not favored for commercial purposes. Stones were used as the printing surface, a cumbersome and expensive method. By the 1850's stones were replaced with metal plates-- first zinc, then copper in the 1890s. After the American Civil War mass production was possible, but it wasn't until after the 1876 Centennial Exposition in Philadelphia, where it received much exposure, that lithography flourished.

Brilliantly colored lithography, nicknamed *chromolithography*, was popular with artists and the public. With color lithography, each color is made on a different plate. Each plate is pressed successively against the printing surface. If the plates are not lined up perfectly, the registration will be off, meaning that the different colors will not be lined up on the print.

Hand made lithography is a versatile process that comes in a wide variety of styles. The following lists some of the significant styles. Often many of the styles were used together:

Pen and ink: These resemble pen and ink drawings

Chalk style or crayon style: This type of lithography resembles a chalk or crayon drawing. Even under the magnification, it looks like a chalk or crayon sketch.

Mezzotint style: This creates a similar style to mezzotint, a form of intaglio printing.

Spatter: The artist could splatter ink on the lithographic plate.

Stipple: Stipple dots were used to create tone, such as to give shading to a person or tree. These could be made by hand or with a spiked roller.

Identifying Lithography

As lithography is made with a flat printing plate, the ink will appear flat on the print. The ink lacks the signatures of prints made with a multi-level plate (The raised ink in intaglio and the hard rim around the ink in relief). The only exception is chromolithography which can have a rim around the ink, as seen under the microscope. This rim appears different. In relief, the dark rim of ink is created by the pressure of the relief printing plate, and the rim is hard and rigid. In chromolithography, the rim is created by the settling of the thin lithographic ink and does not appear as mechanical or rigid.

Screen printing, a process invented about 1890, can resemble lithography. Screen print often has an imprint of the mesh which is used. While the screen printing ink lies flat on the printing surface, under the microscope it often appears more painted on almost like enamel.

Realize that lithography has a wide variety of appearances and applications, and can both be manual and process. Most modern commercial printing is photomechanical lithography. In other words, if you see something simply described as 'a lithograph', it should not be automatically assumed that it is an original print.

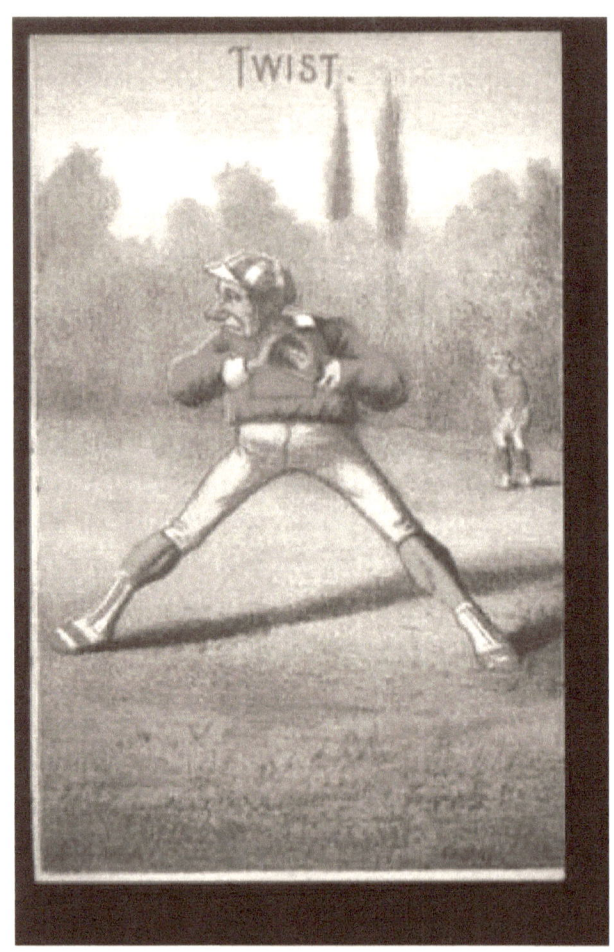

1870s chalk-style lithograph that looks like a chalk sketch

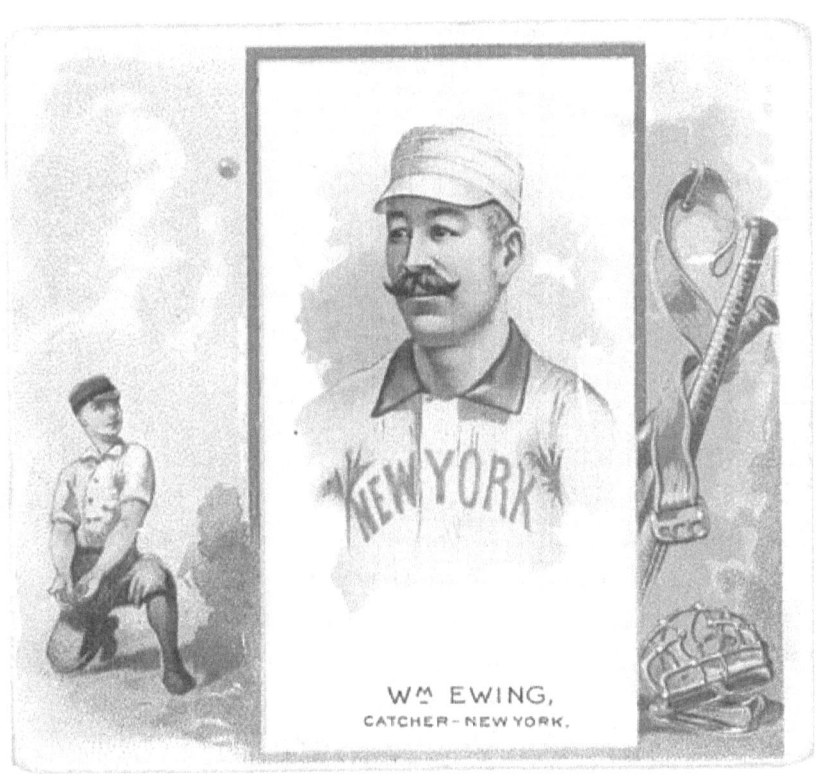

This chromolithograph 1880s tobacco card resembles a watercolor painting

(12)
HAND MADE MISCELLANIOUS PRINTS

This section covers hand made printing processes that do not fit neatly into the categories of relief, intaglio and planography. This section also covers processes that are not printing in the traditional sense, but are popularly included within the genre of fine art prints.

CLICHE-VERRE (GLASS PRINT)

Cliché-verre is not a print in any traditional sense. It is a cross between painting and photography. A glass plate is covered with ink or paint and a design is drawn with a brush or similar. A piece of photographic paper is placed beneath the glass and the glass is exposed to light. The final product is a photograph.

Cliché-verre was popular in the 1800s with such artists as Camille Corot, Theodore Rousseau and Eugene Delacrois. The most prominent 20th century user was Gyorgi Kepes.

MONOTYPE

A monotype is not a print in the traditional sense, and does not require technical printing skill. It is sort of a cross between painting and printing, and is used exclusively in the fine arts. The monotype is made from a flat printing plate. On the printing plate, the artist draws or paints a design in ink. While the ink is wet, a piece of paper is place on top of it and pressure applied, either with a printing press or by hand.

The process is meant to produce a single (mono) print, but there is sometimes enough damp ink left on the plate surface to make a second, weaker, impression. This second impression is called a 'ghost' and can be attractive on its own merit. To add more colors, designs and textures, the monotype might go through several printings from the same plate. As a result, some monotypes are sparse, while others are dense.

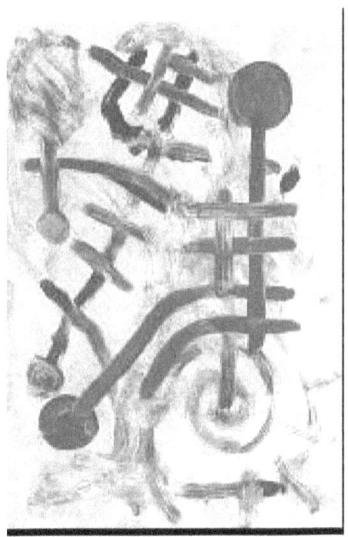

The monotype should not be confused with the monoprint. A monoprint also is a one-of-one print, but made differently. The monoprint is usually made with traditional printing processes, like lithography, etching and woodcut. A monoprint is usually a mixed-media printing, meaning that it involves more that one type of printing and often hand coloring. Even if you can't always remember which is which, you can always remember that, whether monotype or monoprint, the print is unique.

Making Your Own Monotype

There is a wide variety of techniques and styles used in making monotypes. This briefly shows a few common techniques.

Step 1) Get a flat, smooth-surfaced printing plate, like as a sheet of Plexiglas, metal or varnished wood. If you have to you can use cardboard or a rougher board, but the ink will not print as smoothly (which may be an effect you desire).

Step 2) Apply ink to the printer's plate. A roller will make the ink smoother, though you can use a paint brush if you wish. In the following pictures, two color inks were used, but you can use as many or as few colors as you wish. You can use paint instead of ink, but paint often dries quickly which may be a problem if you are slow in creating your design. Go to print and the paint's dry.

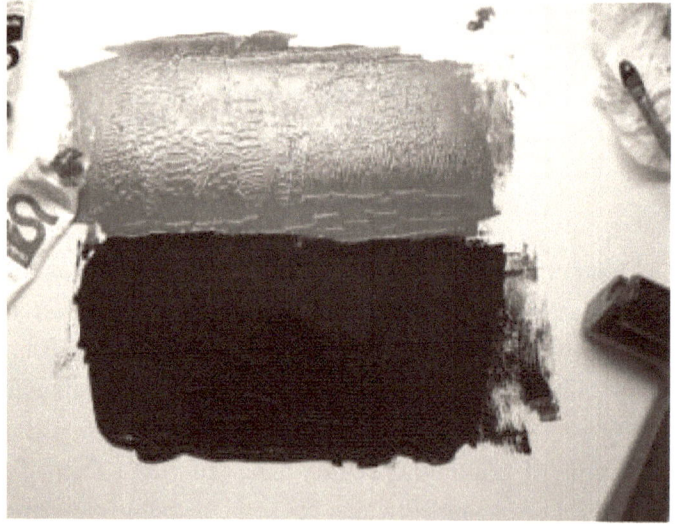

two colors of ink rolled onto the plate

Step 3) Make your design in the ink. If you print before making a design, it will print as a solid ink. Anything you do to the ink now will print as a mark in the solid ink. The simplest way to make a picture is to draw with the blunt end of a brush or pencil.

What is drawn will appear as white and in reverse in the final print. You can also use a brush or paper towel to remove ink for different effects. In the pictures here, I cut out pieces out of paper in the shapes of a boat and a cloud and placed them on the ink. The cloud had ink painted to it to create a different effect. If you want straight borders to your print, you can put tape in a straight line on the edges. You can also make designs in the ink with tape, such as spelling your name.

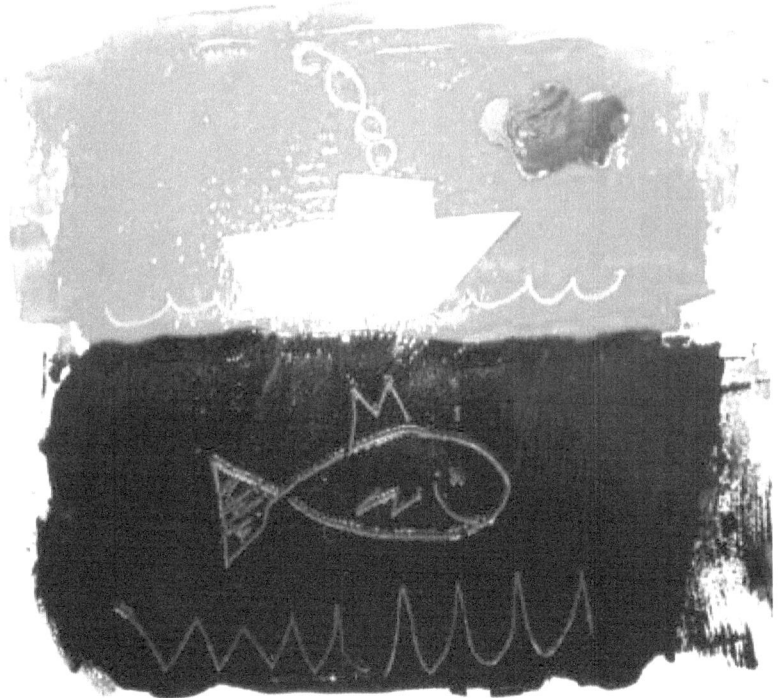

inked printing plate with designs drawn into ink and cutout stencils of boat and cloud

Step 4) Place a piece of paper on top of the ink and apply pressure to the paper. You can apply pressure in a variety of ways, including running your hand or a large spoon over the paper. Make sure to rub all over, so you don't miss a spot. Remove the paper, by slowly pulling from one corner. If you try to lift the paper all at once, it might smudge. Congratulations, you have made your first monotype. If you wish, you can add hand painted details.

Step 5) To make your second, ghost print reprint step 4 with a second piece of paper. You will probably find that this second print is lighter. You may find that you like the ghost better than the first print. Sometimes the ghost turns out to be the better print.

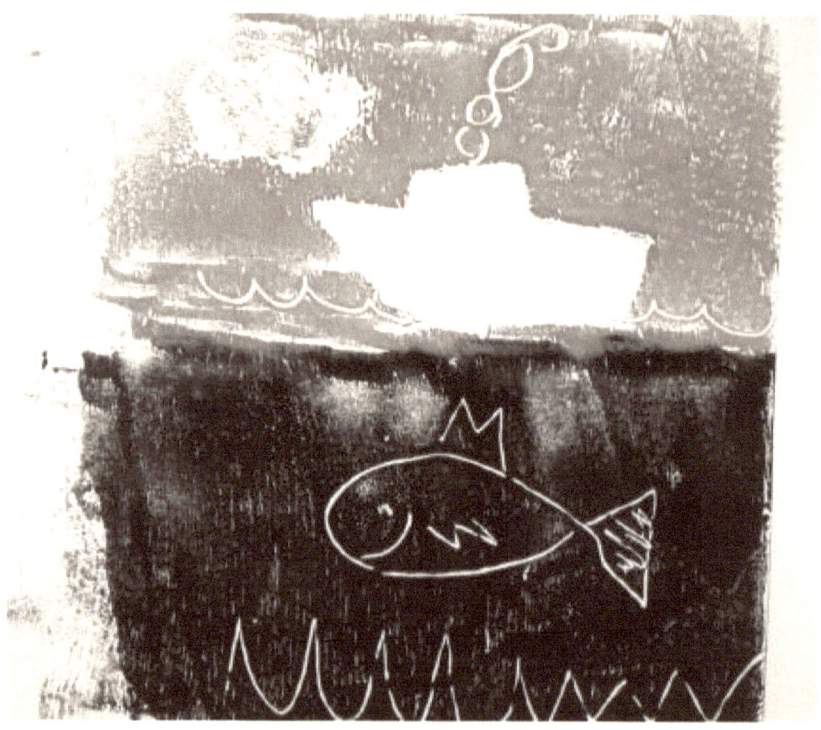

finished print

SCREEN PRINTING, SERIOGRAPHY, SILK SCREEN

Screen printing, also known as serigraphy and silk-screen, is based on stenciling. In stenciling the design is cut out of paper or other material and is then printed by rubbing, rolling, or spraying ink through the cutout areas. Screen printing is a sophisticated stencil process. It was developed about 1890 for advertising. By the 1960 artists were using the process extensively in fine art, giving it the name seriography to sound fancy.

In screen printing a fine mesh, usually silk, is tacked to a wooden frame to serve as a support for a paper stencil. The stencil is glued to the silk. In the basic process, the open mesh of the silk lets the ink through, while the stencil blocks it out. A design can also be blocked out on the screen with glue.

A common method of making a stencil is to cut the stencil with a knife. The artist can also use special peal off material. Another method that is the tusche-and-glue method. The design is inked on the screen with tusche and, when dry, the whole screen is covered with glue. When the glue dries, the design is washed out with kerosene or turpentine. The tusche comes in liquid or crayon form.

Photo-Stencil. Stencil plates can also be made photomechanically. This is called the photo-stencil process and it was invented in 1916. This is not a hand made printing process. Photographically realistic images can be made this way, and these images can be incorporated into screen printing with hand made stencils. Andy Warhol is the most famous user of the photo-stencil.

As the photo-stencil illustrates, a screen print can both be hand made and photomechanical prints. This means that if you see something is described simply as a silkscreen, it should not be automatically assumed that is original print.

Identification: As the mesh does not allow for the fineness of other prints, the screen print is crude relative to other processes. Screen prints can be difficult to distinguish from lithography. As with lithography, the ink is flat on the printing surface, though this flatness is often more pronounced with screen printing. A print can often be identified as a screen print when the pattern of the mesh appears in the ink.

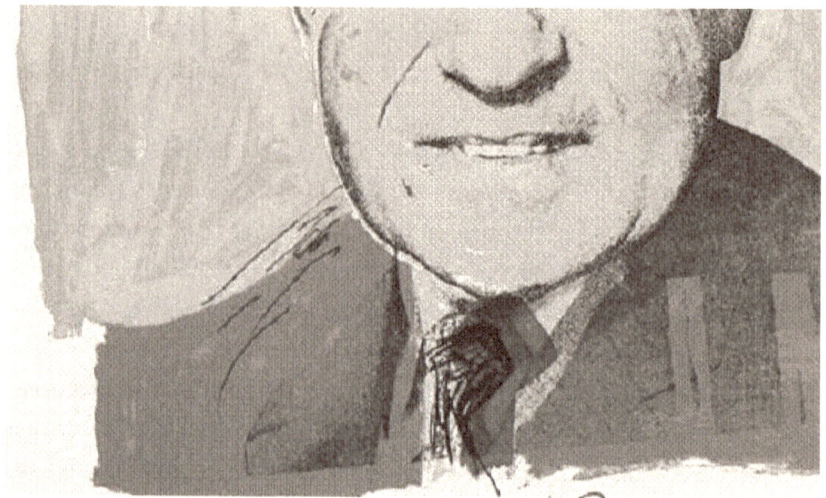

Detail of an Andy Warhol screen print

COLLAGRAPH

A collagraph is a print made from a collage of items glued to a sheet of cardboard, metal or similar flat printing plate. It should not be confused with collatype, which is a type of photomechanical printing commonly used to make postcards in the old days.

The collagraph is primarily used in the fine arts. Pablo Picasso, Juan Gris and Georges Braque were famous practitioners. The collagraph is a relatively modern form of printing, probably originating in the late 1800s.

A wide variety of objects can be attached to the plate to give a wide and wild variety of designs and textures. Common materials include cardboard cutouts, pieces of metal and wood, sand and glue. The collagraph plates can be printed in relief (meaning, the ink is placed on the highest parts), in intaglio (meaning, the ink is placed in the lowest parts) or both. The prints can have a plate mark that is typical to intaglio prints. Collagraphs are often combined with other printing methods, including lithography, woodcut, etching and hand coloring.

Making your own collograph

Collographs are fun, easy and allow for imagination and experimentation. Both kids and adults can make them. As there are so many different materials that can be used, there is almost a limitless variety of styles and designs one can make.

This following example will show you how to make a simple collagraph printed in the relief manner.

Materials
Plate: flat sheet of cardboard, metal,
   wood or similar material
Ink or paint
Glue
Brush or roller for applying ink
Paper to make your print on
Cardboard for making designs to paste to the plate.
Stuff to clean up your mess

Directions
1) Cut out cardboard figures or other designs you want have in your print (trees, dog, clouds, whatever).

2) Glue the cardboard figures onto the plate. Hot glue dries fast. If you use Elmer's glue, you will have to wait a while for it to dry. You can glue other items to the plate if you wish (coins, stones, wood, design in glue). Realize that for proper printing everything has to be of similar height.

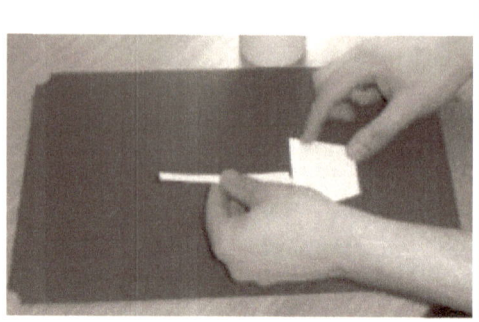
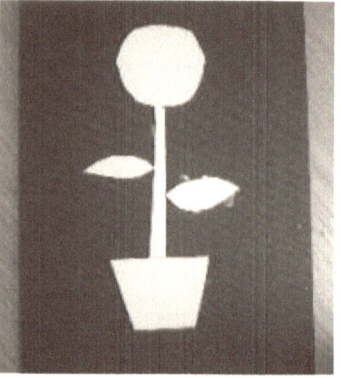

3) With brush and/or roller, apply the ink or paint to the top surface of the items you pasted to the plate.

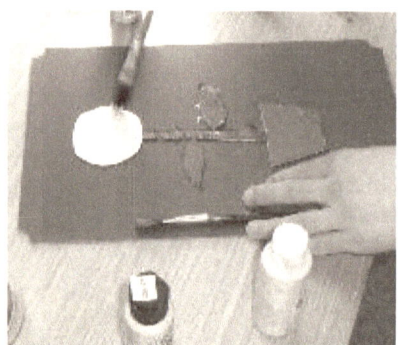
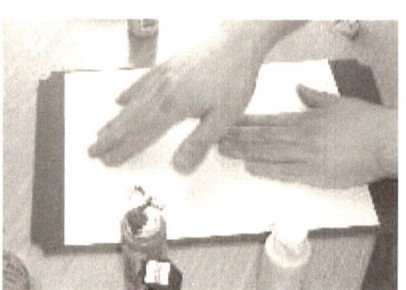

4) Place your piece of printing paper on top of your printing plate. Apply pressure with hand, paper towel other. Remove the paper by carefully pealing it away.

5) You have made a collagraph .If you like your design, you can re-ink your printing plate and make as many prints as you want.

MIXED MEDIA AND MIXED PRINTS PROCESS PRINTS

A mixed media print means that more than one process was used. It is not uncommon for a print to made from two or more forms of printing. A lithograph and woodcut or screen print and engraving may be used together on the same prints. Prints may are also combined with non-printing methods, such as drawing, painting and photography.

The catalogue raisonne should detail which combined printing processes were used.

HAND COLORING

Artists sometimes add color to their prints by painting on an ink-wash or watercolor paint. In general, hand coloring will leave large areas of color but with uneven edges that, in areas, either don't reach or overlap the borders of the print or inside details. As with most watercolor paintings there will be varying densities of ink. This is due to different levels of ink coming off the brush or the brush painting of the same space twice.

(13)
PHOTOMECHANICAL
(NOT HAND MADE) PRINTS

Photomechanical prints are not hand made prints. This printing was designed for the commercial mass reproduction of graphics, including for the printing of soup can labels, glossy magazine covers, advertising signs, calendars and vacation postcards.

Some famous artists make photomechanical reproductions of their original paintings, prints and photographs. Sometimes these reproductions are artist signed and limited edition numbered. These are collectable, they shouldn't be confused with the original hand made prints.

The following is a look at some of the most common forms of photomechanical printing.

* * * *

Halftone Printing

The most common and easily identifiable photomechanical process is the half-tone process. This is the common process used to make reprints and counterfeits of original art. The collector who knows how to identify a half-tone print can identify many fakes and cheap reprints of expensive handmade prints.

The half-tone printing process is one of the most significant inventions of modern times and has been applied to relief, intaglio and lithographic printing. Before the invention of the half-tone process in the 1870s, it was not possible to mechanically print photorealistic images in newspapers and magazines. It was only possible print to newspaper and magazine pictures with handmade prints, like woodcut and engraving. This could create attractive images, but without the subtle tones and detail of a photograph. If you look at the pictures in a 1870s Harper's Weekly or similar publication, you will see the images look like drawings.

The invention of the halftone printing process, often aptly called the dot process, replaced lines with dots, allowing for greater detail. In the process, a photographic image is projected through a special screen, resembling a screen door, and is projected onto a photochemically sensitized printing plate. The screen transforms the image into a series of tiny dots on the printing plate, which then appear in the resulting print. These tiny dots allow for a much finer detail than engravings, etchings and woodcuts. While halftone can't produce the quality and detail of a real photograph, it can make a realistic representation. This process is used today to illustrate newspapers, magazines and books, but also trading cards, advertising signs, postcards, cereal boxes and more. If you take a strong magnifying glass or microscope and look closely at a picture in a magazine on your coffee table you will see that it is made up of tiny dots. For a black and picture the dots will be black. For a color picture, the dots will be various colors.

For many halftone prints, the halftone printing was used only on part of the prints. In the below 1963 baseball card, the player's picture, including uniform, hands and face, is made up of the halftone dots. The border design and text are solid ink. In a magazine, the picture may have the halftone dots, while the article text will be solid ink.

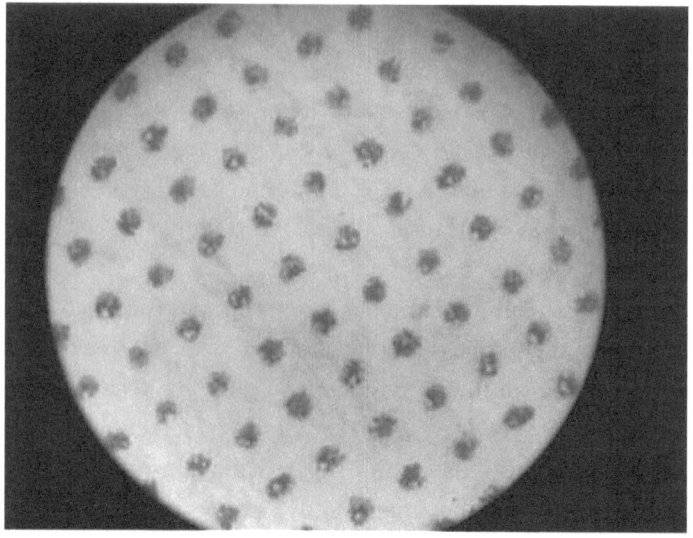

If you see a Durer woodcut or Picasso linoleum cut that is a halftone print, you can be confident that the print is a reprint.

Photolithography

Photolithography is a general term that refers to photomechanical lithography with and without the half-tone process.

Photolithography without halftone can reproduce woodcuts, engravings and other original prints of solid ink. In the 1800s, photolithography was commonly used often used to reproduce maps.

Photolithography without half-tone can closely resembles certain types hand made lithography. Under the microscope, the ink will have the same flat appearance. It cannot reproduce well the subtle tones and detail of hand made wash lithography and hand made crayon and chalk lithography.

Photolithography with and without half-tone has been popular in 20th century commercial printing and is often used together on the same print. As with all halftone printing, it is made up of a fine pattern of color dots. For a black and white print the dots will be one color. For a color print, there will be dots of different colors. Halftone make quality naked eye reproductions of hand made wash, crayon and chalk lithographs, but the fine dot pattern under the magnifying glass will give it away as a reproduction.

Photoengraving

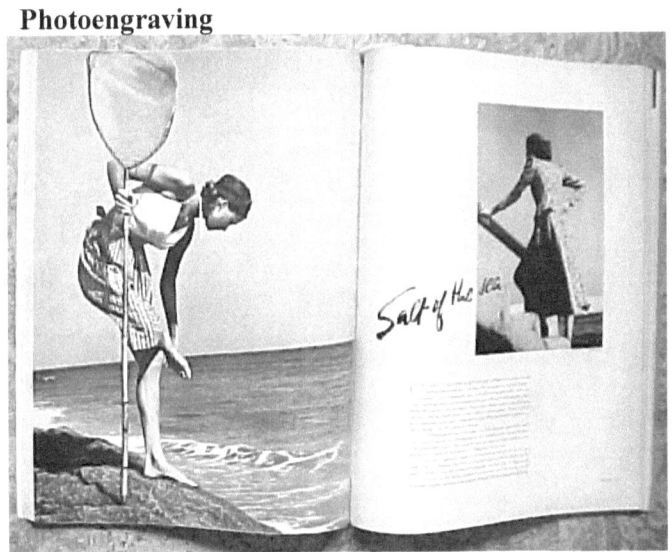

Many vintage magazine pictures are photoengravings

Photoengraving was a vintage commercial printing method. In the late 1800s to mid 1900s, photoengraving was used to make the images for magazines, newspapers, advertising posters and commercial prints. It is rarely used commercially today, having been replaced by photolithography. Photoengraving can reproduce both solid lines and solid areas of ink and the subtle tones of photographs. To reproduce tone, photoengraving uses the halftone dot pattern.

Photoengraving is a relief process. Under a microscope of 50x or more power, photoengraving has the distinct dark rim or edge common to all relief prints. Even the halftone dots of a photoengraving will have the dark rim.

As photoengraving has the rim and can print solid ink when halftone is not used, it can make deceptive reproductions of original woodcuts, wood-engravings and linoleum cuts.

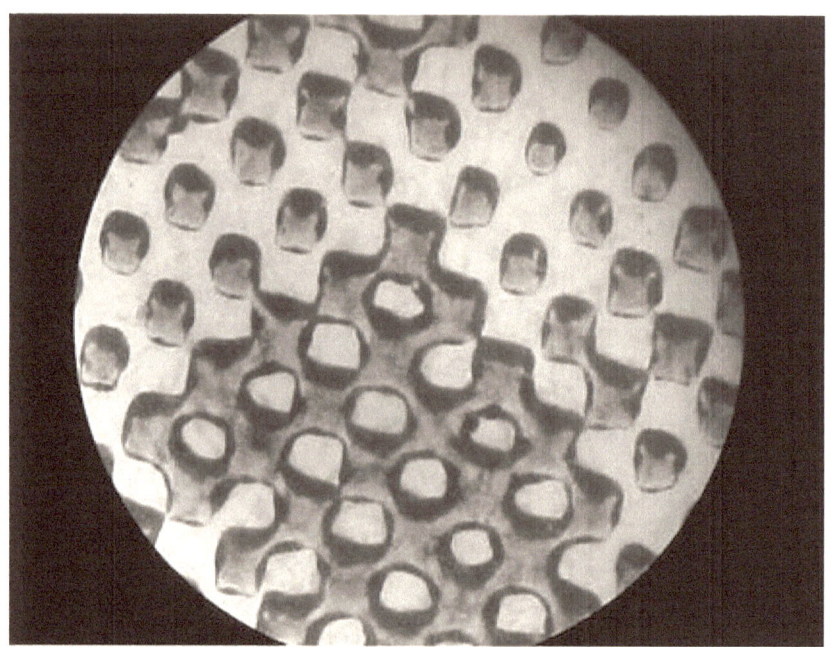

**microscopic view of photoengraving with
the dark edge and waffle-like pattern**

Collotype

Collotype was a photomechanical process popular in the early 20th century. It was versatile and produced high quality images on many types of paper. Some examples can be difficult to distinguish from photographs. Many silent era lobby cards and picture postcards are collotypes. Postcards with "Albertype" printed on back are collotypes.

The images can be in any color and usually have a matte surface. Under the microscope, the ink pattern in the image is reticulated, meaning that it appears like a mosaic with similar size pieces of irregular shapes. Sometimes it resembles a bunch of noodles. Some collotypes were varnished, making it difficult to see the reticulation even under magnification.

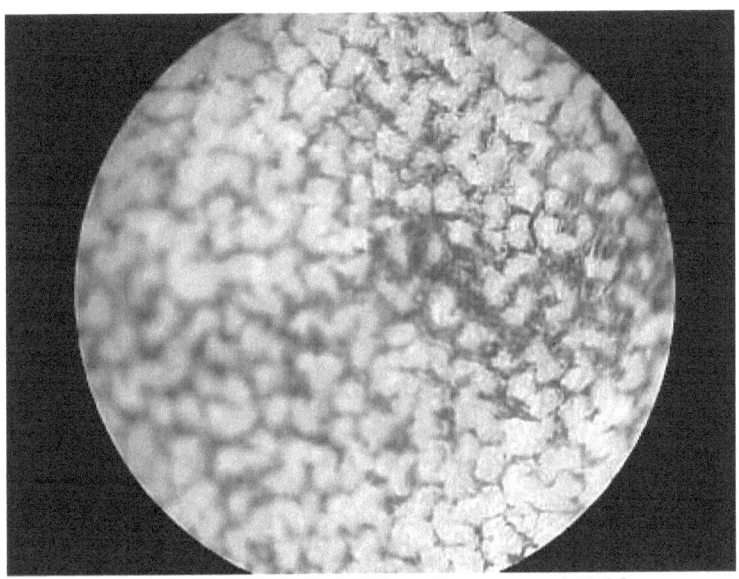

microscopic view of a 1920s collotype movie lobby card showing the distinct reticulated pattern

Photogravure (Gravure)

Photogravure, also known as gravure and rotogravure, is the term for any photomechanical intaglio print.

As with all intaglios, photogravures will often have a plate mark. This means it can make a deceptive reproduction a hand made intaglio print. A plate mark can be missing when it is cut off, which was often the case for commercial prints.

There are several variations to photogravure.

Line photogravure was used to reproduce line images, including etchings and engravings. Many earlier photogravures can be differentiated from the hand made intaglio prints because they reproduced because the photogravure does not have the difference in depth between darker and liner lines. However, with advancements in technology, the photogravure could reproduce these differences. In many cases, it is important to examine the paper to determine if it is a photogravure or hand made intaglio from earlier centuries. Line photogravure was invented in 1827, but was not commonly used until the 1860s and 70s.

Photogravure can also reproduce tonal images . Phorogravure reproductions of photographs is known for its excellent image quality and detail. This 'tonal photogravure' was invented in the late 1800s and is still used today. The surface is matte and the image can come in any color. Vintage photogravure's sometimes have images that are faded and with foxing (browning/reddish age spots. Under the microscope an irregular often speckled ink pattern exists. A variation of the photogravure called the rotary photogravure was produced on a cylinder. The ink on the photogravure image is set up in an even grid with dots of ink surrounded by intersecting white lines. This is a similar pattern to the halftone.

Photogravure was used commercially in the 1800s to mid 1900s. It was used to make commercially sold prints, book plates and pictures for magazines and newspapers. It is rarely used today commercially.

Computer prints

Computer printing is used today in both our normal lives and in the fine arts. While there have been numerous processes used in the past several decades, this section focuses on the two most commonly used: *electrostatic* printing and *ink jet* printing. The popular giclee process is a type of ink jet printing.

Electrographic Printing: Laser Printer, Photocopier and Xerox

Large numbers of reproductions have been made using these printers, all of which use electrostatic or electrographic printing. Under the microscope, the resulting prints are easily identified. The lines are made up of many tiny dust-like grains of pigment that have been fused to the electostically charge area. However, not all the grains make it to the intended area, so the print is identified by the many stragglers outside the lines. It looks like it needs a dusting.

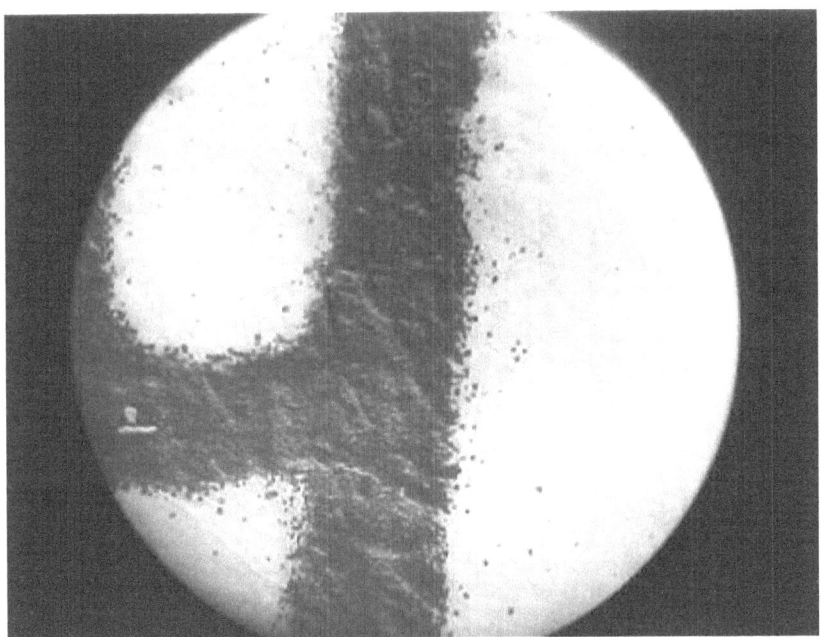

Microscopic view of a laser computer print, showing the unique 'dusty' ink pattern

Inkjet including Giclee

Today's inkjet printer can produce attractive color and black and white reproductions and can be printed on many surfaces. There are a variety of types, all squirting the ink onto paper surface.

Under the microscope, the image is made up of a fine dot pattern closely resembling a halftone lithograph.

The giclee, or iris print, is a fancy type of inkjet printing often used in the fine arts. It can make high quality reproductions of paintings, photographs and prints on a variety of papers, from matte to glossy to canvas. As the images are resistant to fading and deterioration, the process is used to make many limited edition display photographs. Famous artists who have made giclees include Richard Avedon, Walter Chin, Stephen Holland and David Hockney.

(14)
EDITIONS

Fine art prints are often printed in editions. An edition will contain a finite and often known number of prints. There is the normal print run, then there are often additional editions, such as an **Artist's Proof** edition or **Printer's Proof** edition.

The total print run is the sum of all of the editions. *70 regular prints + 20 Artist's Proofs + 14 Printer's Proofs + 10 other prints = 114 total prints.*

Many collectors get a mistaken impression of rarity. They may see a print numbered out of 100 and don't realize that additional and even larger editions of the print exist. A rule of thumb is that prints in the regular edition usually far outnumber each of the other editions.

Artist's proofs and printer's proofs are not to be confused with proofs. Proofs are test prints made before the final print run. For example, the printer or artist may make a proof of a print to see how the design is coming along. Looking at the proof she may decide the print needs more red in the face, or more shading to a tree in the background. Proofs will often differ, if only slightly, from the final product.

Other than perhaps being printed on different paper or having minor printing differences, artist's proofs and printer's proofs are usually identical to the regular prints. Artist's prints are an additional edition meant for artist's personal use, whether to keep, sell on the open market or give away to friends and acquaintances. Printer's proofs are just like artist's proofs, except they are made for the printer.

Other common editions include the following:

Hors D' Commerce. Traditionally, these were prints made before the official print run used as a guide for the printer. In modern times, this term is often simply used as a name for an extra edition. In this modern sense, they are essentially the same as artist's proofs and printer's proofs.

Trial Proof. Traditionally a trial proof was used, in similar fashion as the Hors Commerce, as a guide for the printer. In modern times, they are often a name for an extra edition. They can be the same as the regular edition, or, as demonstrated by Andy Warhol, they can differ in color from the regular edition.

Current fine art print editions are often, though not always, hand numbered and/or signed by the artist, usually in pencil or crayon (ink can be detrimental to a print). This writing is often on the lower border area. Often times, the numbering indicates the number of prints in the edition. For example, an edition may be numbered 1/100, 2/100...., indicating that there are one hundred prints in the edition. Numbering can be found in Arabic (1, 2, 3) and Roman (I, II, III). Unless someone in the know says so, it should not be assumed that the prints are numbered in order of printing (#1/100 is printed first, 3/100 is printed third), because they often aren't. If one edition is numbered and another is not, it is reasonable to assume that the unnumbered had a larger print run. An 'unlimited edition' means there was no specified limit to how many prints there could be, and often means many prints were made.

In addition to possible numbering, prints often have handwritten or printed letters that identify the edition. The regular edition will ordinarily have no extra lettering. Common lettering for other editions are shown below. Most often the letters are next to the numbers, such as 'AP 5/100'

    Artist Proofs: AP or EA
    Printer's Proof: PP
    Hors D' Commerce: HC or HDC

Trial Proof: TP

Some editions are hand signed by the artist, and some or not. The catalogue raisonne usually will detail how an edition is signed, numbered and labeled.

Some prints are plate signed. This means that the artist's signature was made into the printing plate and printed with the rest of the design. In other words a 'plate signed Salvador Dali engraving' does not mean it was autographed (hand signed) by Dali.

Some editions are made a long period, sometimes even decades, after the original printing. These editions are often in different states (see Chapter: *States*). Catalogues raisonne will usually list the dates of all editions. Ordinarily, the earliest editions are the most valuable, especially when the later editions are not authorized or signed by the artist.

To prevent later printing, artists and printers often ruin the printing plate. This is called canceling or striking the plate. Sometimes they will make a print of the defaced plate as evidence that the plate was cancelled.

(15)
STATES

Whether due to wear with use or by the artist's intentional reworking, printing plates can change over time. These changes result in prints in different *states*. These changes may be minor or they may be extensive.

Intaglio plates often wear down during printing, resulting in later state prints that are lighter and with less detail.

Printing plates and prints often went through several states. This is most commonly done during the creation of the printing plate, when the artist makes test prints, or proofs, in order to see how the work is coming. The artist will use the proof to see what additions or changes need to be made to the design.

After the first publication of a print, changes are sometimes made. If areas of an intaglio plate have worn down due to excessive printing, details may have to be put back in. In all types of prints, the text may be changed or the image cropped to suit a different purpose. Artists often feel compelled to embellish or change details of print for later editions.

(16)
PAPER

Having a basic knowledge of paper is important. Many fakes and reprints are identified as the paper is too modern or the wrong type for the print to be an original. This chapter is a brief look at some important types of paper throughout history.

While the type and age of the paper can help determine the authenticity of a print, it is not in and of itself proof. Some forgers use old paper. However, many prints are identified as fakes because the paper used is too modern or otherwise inconsistent with the original. Many catalogues raisonne list the type(s) of paper used for a print.

* * * *

The following are standard types of paper.

Laid paper: Until the 1750s, all paper was laid paper. It was made on a mesh consisting of strong wires about an inch apart, with finer wires laid close together across them. This gridiron pattern can be seen when the paper is held to the light. Today, some writing paper is still laid, though the pattern being more of a decoration.

A paper print from the 1500s or 1600s has to be on laid paper.

Wove paper: About 1755, wove paper was invented. Wove paper is made on a finely woven mesh, so the paper does not have the rigid lines pattern of laid paper. Laid and wove paper are easily differentiated when held to the light. Most of today's paper, including computer printer and typing paper, is wove. No print from before 1750 could be on wove paper.

Rag versus wood pulp. In the early history paper was made from rags. Starting about the mid 1800s, rag pulp began to be replaced by wood pulp. Wood became a popular choice due to the scarcity of rags and because wood pulp paper was cheaper to manufacture. The first successfully made American wood pulp paper was manufactured in Buffalo New York in 1855. By 1860, a large percentage of the total paper produced in the U.S. was still rag paper. Most of the newspapers printed in the U.S. during the Civil War period survived because they were essentially acid-free 100% rag paper, but the newspapers printed in the late 1880s turn brown because of the high acid content of the wood pulp paper. In 1882, the sulfite wood pulp process that is still in use today was developed on a commercial scale and most of the high acid content paper was used thereafter in newspapers, magazines and books.

Counterintuitively, modern paper, especially in books, letters and newspapers, is much more likely to turn brown and brittle than paper from before the American Civil War. For the beginning collector, the paper on an early 1800s print can be surprisingly fresh and white.

* * * *

Chronology of Paper
The following is a brief chronology of paper history. Paper has been traced to about 105 AD China. It reached Central Asia by 751 and Baghdad by 793, and by the 14th century there were paper mills in several parts of Europe.

105: Paper making invented in China.
106: First paper cut.

400: Invention of true ink in China.

610: Papermaking introduced to Japan from China.

770: The earliest instance of text printing upon paper, in China.

868: Earliest printed book, the Diamond Sutra, in China.

900: First use of paper in Egypt.

1228: First use of paper in Germany.

1282: Watermarks first used in Europe.

1319: Earliest use of paper money in Japan.

1450-55 Johan Gutenberg's forty two line Bible produced.

1470: First paper poster, in the form of a bookseller's advertisement.

1521: First use of rice straw in Chinese paper.

1589-91 European printing introduced to China and Japan.

1609: First newspaper with regular dates (Germany)

1662: First English newspaper introduced

1869: The first 'Dutch Gilt' papers made in Germany.

1750: Cloth backed papers introduced. Used for maps, charts, etc.

1755: Wove paper introduced

1758: First forgery of bank notes

1763: First Bible printed in American using American paper.

1800-10s: Practical paper making machines developed

1824: First machine for pasting sheets of paper together is introduced. Cardboard is first formed.

1830: Sandpaper introduced commercially.

1830s: Coated paper introduced. This paper is usually coated with China clay, which makes it white and smooth, sometimes glossy. It is most often used in art and illustrated books.

1842: Christmas card invented.

1844: First commercial paper boxes made in America.

1854: Paper made from chemical wood pulp patented.

1862: Tracing paper introduced commercially

1871:Roll toilet paper introduced.

1875:First instance in U.S. of paper coated on both sides.

1903: Corrugated cardboard introduced. Replaced many wooden boxes.

1905: Glassine paper introduced

1906: Paper milk-bottles introduced

1909: Kraft paper introduced
1910: Bread and fruit wrapped in printed paper

* * * *

Some common fine art paper terms

Blind stamp: an embossed sealed used to identify the artist, publisher, printer or collector.

China Paper: a soft paper made in China from bamboo fiber.

Chine appliqué or chine collé: A chine appliqué is a print in which the image is pressed into a thin sheet of China paper which is backed by a thicker and stronger paper. Some proof prints are chine appliqués.

Cold pressed: A paper with slight surface texture made by pressing the finished paper between cold cylinders. In between rough and hot pressed papers.

Deckle edge: the rough, feathery edge on hand made paper.

Deckle Stain: Paper that has a coloring or darkness around the deckle edge.

Drystamp: blindstamp.

Embossment: A physically raised or depressed design in the paper.

Enameled paper: any coated paper..

Glassine paper: A super smooth, semi-transparent paper that is often used to make the envelopes that hold stamps

Hand made Paper: Paper made by hand in individual sheets.

Hot Pressed: A paper surface that is smooth. Made by pressing a finished paper sheet through hot cylinders.

India paper: an extremely thin paper used primarily in long books to reduce the bulk.

Machine Made Paper: Made on a machine called a "Fourdrinier." Produces consistent shape and textured paper.

Marbling: a decorative technique of making patterns on

paper

Mouldmade Paper: paper that simulates hand made paper, but is made by a machine.

Parchment: An ancient form of paper made out of animal skin. It is smooth and semi-translucent

Plate Finish: A smooth surface made by a calendar machine.

Rag Paper: Made from non-wood fibers, including rags, cotton linters, cotton or linen pulp.

Rough: a heavily textured paper surface

Tooth: A slight surface texture.

Vellum: a modern version of parchment, with the same dense, animal skin-like appearance. A slightly rough surface and is semi-translucent. Some drafting paper is called vellum.

Velox: Black and white paper print for proofing or display.

* * * *

Watermarks

For centuries paper manufacturers have often distinguished their product by means of watermarks. A watermark is a design in paper made by creating a variation in the paper thickness during manufacture. The watermark is visible when the paper is held up to a light. Watermarks can sometimes give important information about the age of the paper and the authenticity of the print.

Watermarks are known to have existed in Italy before the end of the 13th century. Two types of watermark have been produced. The more common type, which produces a translucent design when held up to a light, is produced by a wire design laid over and sewn onto the sheet mold wire (for hand made paper) or attached to the "dandy roll" (for machine-made paper). The rarer "shaded" watermark is produced by a depression in the sheet mold wire, which results in a greater density of fibers--hence, a shaded, or darker, design when held up to a light. Watermarks are often used commercially to identify the manufacturer or the grade of paper. They have also been used to detect and prevent counterfeiting and forgery.

Catalogues raisonne often list watermarks used or otherwise discuss watermarks as it relates to the artists' work.

Examples of how watermarks help identify prints:
If a Salvador Dali print has a watermark consisting of the word "ARCHES" with an infinity sign (sideways '8') beneath, the print is a fake. Dali used ARCHES brand paper, but in 1980 ARCHES added the infinity sign to the watermark. 1980 was past Dali's working career and Dali himself stated that he never used the 'infinity' paper. While this watermark is easily identified, some enterprising forgers and dealers, picked the 'infinity' paper where the watermark was near an edge so they could conveniently cut off the infinity. A simple rule of thumb for collectors, is to make sure that you buy a Dali print on Aches paper where the watermark is entirely on the paper and away from an edge.

For John James Audubon's large size "Birds of America" prints, the presence of a "J. Whatman" watermark is strong evidence that the print is original. No known reprints or later restrikes are on paper with that watermark.

Pablo Picasso sometimes used paper with his personal watermark.

(17)
LONGWAVE BLACK LIGHT:
A TOOL FOR IDENTIFYING
MANY REPRINTS AND FAKES

For collectors of Pre World War II paper material—whether it's fine art prints, photographs, theatre programs, movie posters, trading cards or postcards— there is a sophisticated yet inexpensive and easy to use tool for quickly identifying many modern reprints and fakes. This tool is called a longwave black light. While there are many uses for black light in collecting and beyond, this chapter introduces how it can be used to identify modern paper.

How Black Light Works
A black light allows the collector to see things not seen under normal daylight. Ultraviolet light is outside the human's visible spectrum, meaning that it cannot be seen by human eyes. However, in a dark room, different materials can fluoresce (glow in the dark) under black light. Most of us have experienced black lights that make the whites on our shirts or shoes glow brightly. Some materials fluoresce brightly, some not at all and the rest somewhere in between. Fluorescence can differ in color. Some inks fluoresce yellow, some brown and some blue. This quality of fluorescence happens at the atomic level of the material.

Identification of Modern Papers Using Black Light
A black light is effective in identifying of many, though not all, modern paper stocks.

Starting in the late 1940s, manufacturers of many products

began adding optical brighteners and other new chemicals to their products. Optical brighteners are invisible dyes that fluoresce brightly under ultraviolet light. They were used to make products appear brighter in normal daylight, which contains some ultraviolet light. Optical brighteners were added to laundry detergent and clothes to help drown out stains and to give the often advertised `whiter than white whites.' Optical brighteners were added to plastic toys to makes them brighter and more colorful. Paper manufacturers joined the act as well, adding optical brighteners to many, though not all of their white papers stocks.

A black light can identify many trading cards, posters, photos and other paper items that contain optical brighteners. In a dark room and under black light optical brighteners will usually fluoresce a very bright light blue or bright white. To find out what this looks like shine a recently made white trading card, snapshot or most types of today's printing paper under a black light.

If paper stock fluoresces very bright as just described, it almost certainly was made after the mid 1940s and after the early 1950s if it's a photograph. It is important to note that not all modern papers will fluoresce this way as optical brighteners are not added to all modern paper. For example, many modern wirephotos have no optical brighteners. This means that if a paper doesn't fluoresce brightly this does not mean it is necessarily old. However, with few exceptions, if a paper object fluoresces very brightly, it could not have been made before World War II.

It is important that the collector gain practical experience. This means using a black light to examine and compare the fluorescence of a variety of items.

Where to buy a black light
Black lights are widely available and have a wide variety of

uses. Geologists use them to identify rocks, collectors of glass uses them for authentication. They are even used to find scorpions at night. Black lights are sold by many science, hobby or rock stores. I bought mine and tested it out at a hobby store in my home town.

They can also be purchased online. I have seen adorable hand-held models offered for at amazon.com and eBay.

You should buy a longwave black light as opposed to a shortwave black light. Shortwave is important in certain specialty areas, like stamps and gem stones, but longwave is the safest and all you need for the prints discussed in this guide. Longwave black lights are safe for normal collector's use, but you should read the safety instructions that come with the light.

(18)
ARTIST'S SIGNATURE

Artists sometimes sign their prints, usually on numbered limited editions. The signature is ordinarily on the bottom border and in pencil or crayon. Pen ink can bleed into art paper.

Hand signing prints is a relatively modern phenomenon, started in the 1800s. Durer and other earlier artists had their monogram printed as part of the graphics. This printing press printed signature is called 'signed in the plate' or 'plate signed.' The catalogues raisonne will usually indicate which prints were hand signed and which were plate signed.

In cases, a print of a celebrity has both the signature of the celebrity and the artist. This is the case with some Andy Warhol screen prints, including prints of Mick Jagger, Wayne Gretzky and Pete Rose. Many prints by sports artist Leroy Neiman are signed by both Neiman and the athlete. The purchaser of the print often got the athlete's signature at an autograph show or private signing.

A hand signature does not in and of itself prove a print original. Many modern artists were celebrities during their lifetime and were asked by fans to sign reprint posters, postcards, books, photos and even baseballs. As with all celebrities, artists' signatures have been and will be forged.

The collector can get a general feel for what an artist's or celebrities autograph looks like, and can use the catalogue raisonne to know which prints were originally signed and where and which were not. With experience, the collector will be able to identify many bad mistakes. However, signature authentication takes great experience and expertise and should be left to experts.

The following are well known experts who issue LOAs for autographs. These companies will make mistakes from time to time, can are offering experienced opinions. The expert art dealer, historian or auctioneer who specializes in the artist will usually have a good eye for the artist's signature.

University Archives/John Reznikoff: universityarchives.com
PSA/DNA: www.psadna.com
Bob Eaton/R & R Enterprises rrauction.com
Mike Gutierrez Authentication: www.mgauction.net
James Spence Authentication www.spenceloa.com
Onlineauthentics.com
International Autograph Collectors Club and Dealers Association (IACC-DA) and UACC are reputable autograph organizations who's member dealers must adhere to strict rules including having lifetime guarantees of authenticity.

Remember that the above companies give LOAs for the autograph only. Most are not offering opinions on the print itself. They will give a LOA for an Andy Warhol signed Time magazine cover if they feel the autograph is real.

(19)
DEAL WITH QUALITY SELLERS

No matter whether you are buying expensive fine art prints or autographed footballs, it is important to deal with quality sellers. A quality seller is knowledgeable, experienced, honest and reliable. Some top dealers are also the top experts in their field.

The more knowledgeable you are about prints, the more you will be able to judge the seller by reading their auction or sales descriptions. If the seller's description and pictures of an Andy Warhol screen prints match up with the listing in the online Warhol catalog raisonne, you will be able to say that it appears that the seller deals with legitimate items. In other cases, it will be clear the seller has no idea what he's talking about.

The following websites are good places to look for dealers.

The Art Dealers Association of America
    www.artdealers.org

International Fine Print Dealers Association (IFPDA)
    www.printdealers.com

The IFPDA is a non-profit group that accepts as members dealers who meet strict criteria. Each dealer is required to guarantee the authenticity and provide a detailed description of the work sold.

The IFPDA also sponsors prints fairs in different parts of the country. These are shows where dealers show their prints and collectors can view and purchase. It's a great way to view a variety of prints, old to new.

Beyond knowledge level and what groups they belong to, good dealers are reliable about shipping, returns and fixing legitimate problems when they arise. Even if a known reliable seller specializes in vintage hockey equipment or gumball machines, you will at least know that if a problem arises he will accept returns.

A good way to discover good sellers is to ask fellow collectors. Many collectors also discover reliable seller by purchasing one or two inexpensive items and seeing how the transaction works.

(20)
PROVENANCE

Provenance is where an item came from. Who made it, who were the owners and sellers, who else significant handled it along the way. Good documented provenance helps establish the authenticity of a print.

Documentation of provenance can include sales receipts, letters about ownership and history, magazine and newspaper articles and auction catalogs. Provenance can include an expert's letter of authenticity.

Provenance does not in and of itself authenticate a print, but it can be an integral part of authentication. It is a piece in the puzzle. If a print matches the catalogue raisonne and is the correct type of paper and printing, that it comes with a sales receipt from an prominent auction house or respected gallery will only make you more confident about the authenticity.

A practical example of good provenance is buying from a well known and respected dealer or auction house. This is making your own good provenance. The fact that a top dealer believes the print to be genuine is significant— especially if you, as an experienced collector, agree with her verdict. Save the receipt or other documentation of sale. When you turn to resell the photo, you will have documentation that it came from a reliable source.

The less knowledgeable you are about a print and artist, the more important the seller and provenance.

Judging the provenance requires that you be knowledgeable about who are reputable and who are not reputable sellers and auction houses and letter of authenticity (LOA) writers. For a

Salvador Dali, an LOA from internationally renown Dali Expert Albert Field is considered substantial proof of authenticity. On the other hand, a LOA from your local Xerox repairman will not hold the same weight.

The collector can obtain a letter of authenticity from recognized authorities on an artist. The following are four prominent organizations. A LOA from any one of these organizations is significant evidence of authenticity.

Salvador Dali: Salvador Dali Archives:
www.daliarchives.com This group was founded by the famous Dali expert Albert Field (died 2003). Dali himself approved of this group. For an authentic piece, Field would give an LOA and stamp and sign the back.

Andy Warhol: The Andy Warhol Foundation for the Visual Arts. www.warholfoundation.org
This institution was set up by Warhol's will and offers opinions of authenticity on Warhol's work. Upon examination, they stamp the back of the work of art and issue a letter of opinion.

Roy Lichtenstein: The Roy Lichtenstein Foundation www.lichtensteinfoundation.org

Leroy Neiman: Knoedler Publishing
www.leroyneiman.com
Knoedler is the artist's publisher and representative.

Be aware that provenance can be faked or embellished. For every forged Rembrandt painting or George Washington autograph there is a made up story of where it came from.

Do you know why I like honest sellers? Because they're honest. If a seller you know to be honest says he got the photograph signed by Frank Sinatra in a Chicago hotel elevator, you know the seller got the photograph signed by Frank Sinatra in a Chicago hotel elevator. If he says he purchased the print from Sotheby's, you know the print came from Sotheby's.

(21)
WHAT IS AN ORIGINAL PRINT?

Most people have a good idea what is original and what is not. I don't have to explain to anyone that a Xerox copy of the Mona Lisa isn't original. There are, however, gray areas and areas of different legitimate points of view.

An original print is a print where the graphics are brand new at the time it was made. It is not a reproduction or copy of something that existed before.

Traditionally, only hand made prints were been considered original prints. In fact, hand made prints are often referred to as 'original prints.' I don't use the term that way as a handmade print can copy another print and that's not originality.

Most photomechanical prints reproduce another image and these are rightly not called original. There are, however, cases were a photomechanical print can be considered original. For example, a handmade print may incorporate photomechanical printing or a collage may juxtapose a number of photomechanical images in unique way. Many of us have computer graphics programs that allow us to sketch a brand new design by moving the mouse or our finger across the touch pad.

Most, not all, original prints are hand made prints, and most photomechanical prints, not all, are not original prints.

An original print by a famous artist is an original print where the printing plate was made by the artist and the printing was done or closely supervised/approved by the artist. While artists often have assistants who help in the preparing of the plate and the printing, an original Picasso can't have been made without Picasso's approval or awareness.

There will be debates about how involved an artist was in the making of a particular print. If the artist *telephoned it in* and his assistants did most of the work, many collectors will not consider the work an original of the artist, or at least entirely by the artist.

Artists sometimes take the original printing plate and print a new edition from this plate years later. Sometimes the later prints will be different, perhaps in new colors and/or different states. Some collectors consider these later prints to be originals, while others do not. Either way, later prints made by the artist often have strong financial value, in particular when the prints have short limited editions and are artist signed and numbered.

Sometimes the printing plates exist after the artist's death and are used to make more prints. These prints are not original, though some of these restrikes have some value if antique and rare.

Some famous artists have made photomechanical reproductions of their paintings. If limited edition and artist signed, these reproductions can have value, but are not original.

(22)
MAKING THE FINAL OPINION

There is no equation for determining authenticity. To make a judgment you should take into consideration a variety of qualities and factors. Avoid using just one quality to make a judgment, such as looking only at the paper or only at the provenance. Looking at just one quality can lean to an erroneous conclusion. If a 2005 forger make a computer print on a 300 year old sheet of laid paper, you would incorrectly judge the age of the printing if you looked only at the paper.

A good judgment should take into consideration the following types of, if not exact, questions.

What do you know about the artist's prints? Were the artist's prints commonly reprinted or faked over the years, and what do the reprints or fakes look like? Do you know who are the experts on the artist?

Is the print listed in a catalogue raisonne and how does the print match the catalogue listing (size, numbering, etc)?

What is the documented provenance? This includes past sales, the current seller, letter of authenticity, etc. Does this documentation show or at support that the print is authentic?

Is the print on the correct paper, or at least on paper consistent with the correct? For example, if the print is supposed to be from 1500s, the paper should be laid.

Is the paper inconsistent with the print being original? If the paper is wove or fluoresces under black light, the print couldn't be an original Albrecht Durer.

Is the printing correct, or at least consistent with being correct? If the print is supposed to be an engraving, does it have a plate mark and the general appearance of an engraving?

Is the printing clearly inconsistent with the print being an original? If the original is a linoleum cut, a halftone dot pattern would show it's a reprint.

Don't forget to get a second opinion if you need or will feel safer with one.

What is the seller's authenticity guarantee, return policy and reliability? When you know you can return an expensive print for a refund if it turns out to be a fake, answering the previous questions are not so life and death.

David Rudd Cycleback is an art historian specializing in the issues of authenticity.   He is also author of *Judging the Authenticity of Photographs*, *Judging the Authenticity of Early Baseball Cards*, *Beginner's Guide to Ultraviolet Light and Longwave Blacklight* and *Conceits/Understanding Visual Illusions.*

www.ingramcontent.com/pod-product-compliance
Lightning Source LLC
Chambersburg PA
CBHW030907180526
45163CB00004B/1746